I0149736

AUTOBIOGRAPHY OF "HAWKIE."

THE RATTLE O' THE BANE. (See page 51).

HAWKIE

THE AUTOBIOGRAPHY OF A GANGREL

EDITED BY

JOHN STRATHESK

> The Gangrel, on his timmer pegs,
> Wha, through the day, for awmous begs ;
> At night, will dance on twa gude legs
> And—Whistle ower the lave o't.
>> —*Charles Gray.*

GLASGOW:
DAVID ROBERTSON & CO.
EDINBURGH: OLIVER & BOYD.   PAISLEY: ALEX. GARDNER.

———

1888.

PREFACE

~~~~~~~~

Ae nicht at e'en a merry core
   O' randie gangrel bodies,   (*Vagrants.*)
In Poosie Nansie's held the splore   (*Merry-making*)
   To drink their orra duddies.   (*Odd clothing.*)

He was a care-defying blade
   As ever Bacchus listed,
Though Fortune sair upon him laid
   His HEART she ever missed it.
          —"*The Jolly Beggars* " (BURNS.)

TO those who knew Scotland well, especially Glasgow and the West, during the first half of this century, the following pages will vividly recall the old, thin, lame, dust-begrimmed, poorly-clad figure of William Cameron, *alias* " Hawkie," Beggar, Street Orator, and Wit. For, despite his inveterate love of the " dram," and his furnishing, in other respects, a living illustration of Burns' line, " Nae farther we can fa'," his biting sarcasm, reckless wit and snell " hits," made him a general favourite. Hawkie's last joke or smart *repartee* was passed on as eagerly as the " Latest Telegram " of the present day, and was spoken of by merchants as " worth a small fortune on the north journey." Every book of Scottish stories, from " THE LAIRD O' LOGAN " downwards, has Hawkie's telling retorts or stinging witticisms as its choicest bits; these, it is not at all the purpose of this volume to reproduce or collect, although they would make a unique and remarkable book.

The Editor can vouch for the following pages being as literal a copy as could be taken from the original manuscript, the genuine production of Hawkie's own hand and brain, written while he was a winter inmate of the 'Glasgow Town's Hospital between 1840-1850, and evidently intended for the press, as, in page 26, he speaks of " the intention of this publication." It was also written under considerable difficulties, for he wrote with his left hand, and, to quote from his letters (see Appendix pages), " My dask is the botetm of a window, and writes standing on the left foot." . . . " For the narrative, if I go beyond truth, I am aware, that it would mak me the loast character in existance, as every town and village in my perigreenations can judge for itself, as for what has taken pleas between me and my congregations on the street. I am, in general, drunk when they happen, and I do not commit them to memory."

"Hawkie" wrote the Autobiography at the request of the late Mr David Robertson, Her Majesty's Bookseller, and a kind friend to the poor waif. The laborious task of deciphering and transcribing it, has been admirably done by Mr Robert Donaldson, whose recollections of " Hawkie " are numerous, accurate, and vivid; and,—with the exception of some changes in spelling, &c., necessary for the comfort of the reader, and some *spicy* bits here and there, which the Editor, falling back on Hawkie's own expression, and applying to it the standard of to-day, has excluded, as "contrary to the intention of this publication,"—the book is practically a genuine reproduction of Hawkie's original manuscript.

To elderly readers, the book will recall the "Edie Ochiltrees," and beggars of long past years, of one of whom (Andrew Gemmell), Sir Walter Scott, in his introduction to "The Antiquary," tells, that, when a laird told him "he had no silver in his pocket, or he would have given him sixpence." "I can give you change for a note, Laird," said Andrew. The same worthy lamented the degradation of his craft. He said, "as a trade it was £40 a year worse since he first practised it. Begging was in *modern* times scarcely the profession of a gentleman; and that, if he had twenty sons, he would not easily be induced to breed one of them up in his own line."

While few will regret that such vagrants are largely things of the past, many will welcome this volume as a matter-of-fact Gazetteer of Scotland from a beggar's point of view, and recognise, in Hawkie's pithy prose, full length portraits of the "Sodger," "the Tousie Drab," "the Tinkler hizzie," "the Raucle Carlin," "the Sturdy Caird," "the Poor gut-scraper," and other characters so graphically described in Burns' racy and dramatic poem *The Jolly Beggars;* whilst all will be convinced by its perusal of the great evils of promiscuous alms-giving, sometimes miscalled—CHARITY.

THE EDITOR.

December 1887.

CONTENTS.

AUTOBIOGRAPHY OF "HAWKIE."

CHAPTER I.

EARLY YEARS.

I WAS born at a place called Plean, in the parish of St Ninians, in the shire of Stirling, where my mother's forbears were residenters for generations unknown, although I can only trace them to the days of Charles the Second. The name of my mother was Paterson, her mother's name was Square. She was the daughter of Ellshander, or Alexander Square, the companion of John Balfour of Burley in his Covenanting campaigns ; My father's name was Dugald Cameron, he came from a place called Braemar; his mother's name was Stewart. The earliest account I can give of my grandmother's connections is only that she had a brother hanged about the borders of Lochaber, for the supposed murder of a man of the name of Campbell, who was King's factor in that district for the estates confiscated at the rebellion of 1715-45.

If we can believe a Highland account, my grandfather, whose name was Donald Cameron, was no far distant connection of the unfortunate Lochiel. Be that as it may, he held a commission under Lochiel in the Cameron ranks in the rebellion for Prince Charlie, and conducted the forlorn hope at the taking of the city of Edinburgh; he fought in the unfortunate cause of Charles at Prestonpans, Falkirk, and Culloden, where he fell in a charge against Baillie's regiment, in which charge the Camerons suffered sore.

I never saw any of his connections except a sister and a brother, whom my father did not make very welcome. I was but young when the sister visited us. She went to the church with my father and mother, and, when she came home, remarked that their minister preached with a white gown. My father gave her the hint to say no more, and my mother did not understand it.

The brother stayed only one night, my father and he did not seem to agree; my uncle spoke mostly in Erse, which none of us understood, but the English of it was, that he stamped his foot and shook his neive in my father's face, telling him that " he was no man to deny that he was with Charles, and to turn his back on his religion;" which led me to think that my father had been at Culloden at any rate, but as for religion, I do not think that he knew anything about it till he came to the low country. My grandmother had to fly from her house, and, with seven children at her feet, sat in the shelf of a rock watching all her movables carried off, and her house burned by the King's army.

When my father did cast up, all she could do for him was to " cow his heid," and send him to the Low Country to seek service at the Fair of Cockhill, near Callander. He was hired into a religious family of the name of Whitehead, at a place called Pattens on the estate of Tough, in the parish of St Ninian's, where he remained for a number of years; to this family he was indebted for all the learning and religion which he possessed. They were adherents of the Burgher religious body, and took him to church with themselves. He remained serving on the estate of Tough, but with different masters, until he was married, when he got an engagement as servant on the estate of Sauchie in the same parish. His wife had four daughters and one son. Falling into a state of decline, from which she died, she left my father with his small family, and her infant son at the breast, which reduced him to great poverty. About two years after her death he married my mother, who at that time was well advanced in years, and with her he removed to the place where I was born.

My father was engaged as mashman at a distillery called Sauchieferry; he was very poor, and my mother, during harvest, went to the shearing with neighbouring farmers, leaving me in the charge of a girl not six years of age. At such an age she could not be expected to take care of herself; to her I have no grudge, but during that harvest, my right leg caught damage, and left me a cripple for life. It would have been better if my mother had kept her house, as, during that harvest, she lost more than she gained. My father removed back to Sauchie, and took a house in the village of Charterhall, where I was brought up, and where my father and mother terminated their earthly career.

Being lame, I was a heavy charge on my mother during my infant years. At the age of four I was put to school; the teacher was an old decrepit man, who had tried to be a nailer, but at that employment he could not earn his bread. He then attempted to teach a few children, but for this undertaking he was quite unfit; writing and arithmetic were to him secrets as dark as death, and as for English, he was short-sighted, and a word of more than two or three syllables was either passed over, or it got a term of his own making. At this school I continued four years, and was not four months advanced in learning, although I was as far advanced as my teacher.

I was taken from that school and sent to another place called Milton, about a mile distant? this was another *do-no-better* teacher, only he could write, which was his master-piece; his knowledge in arithmetic, although he pretended more, did not exceed the three common rules, and his English was much the same as my former teacher's. At this school I lost another five years, and all my advance in learning was writing and arithmetic, consisting of the three common rules; and he racked our memories learning psalms, chapters of the Bible, and catechisms, till a few of us could begin at the Song of Solomon, and, by heart, go on to the end of Malachi; we also knew by heart the Shorter, Mother's, Brown's, Proofs, and Synod's catechisms, till our little judgments were so mixed up, that, in a few years, I could not answer a question in any of them. All this time was lost, the scholar robbed of his learning, and the parents of their money, through the teacher being ashamed to say " he could go no further."

By this time my father had purchased a steading for a house and yard, and built a house on it, which was lucky for him, as, only a few years after, while hauling a tree in the neighbourhood, it fell on his body, injuring him so much that his recovery was a miracle, and leaving him unable to

earn his bread. When I was twelve years of age, I was
bound apprentice to a tailor in Stirling. As that trade did
not suit my disposition, I entered upon it with reluctance,
and continued about five months when, by a pretended dulness of judgment, I made my master as tired of me as I was
of him, although I knew more of the trade than he suspected.

At last I made off, but durst not go home, and started by
the way of Gargunnock. After lying two nights on the roadside, and suffering cold and hunger, a woman, with whom a
tailor from Kippen was working, took me home with her. I
told her a lot of lies, "that my father was a tailor, and was
dead;" she felt deeply for me and insisted on the tailor,
whose name was Miller, taking me as his man, which he did.
I continued with him six or seven months before I was found
out, receiving 4d. a-day, Miller charging 1s. for himself and
8d. for me. Miller was a "whip-the-cat" (a tailor working
from house to house), and thought nothing of going four
miles in a morning to work at a customer's house, and returning home at night.

This did not suit me over well, but during the summer I.
put up with it. At last a crisis arrived; some men employed
by a locksmith named Macgregor, and myself, were in the
habit of having some fun with an old smith, whose name
I forget. He went by the name of Andrew Brochen; on
him we were wont to play tricks. Andrew had a daughter,
a decent-looking lass. One of the blacksmiths, named Bisland,
got Brochen's daughter into the smiddy, and after working a
deal of mischief, pulled down the bellows, and a game-cock
of Brochen's happened to be killed. When Brochen returned
I was standing outside the door, which I had locked for fun;
when he opened the door and found his daughter inside with
a man, his cock killed, and the bellows broken, he declared
there was more damage done, and employed a writer in
Kippen, named Grahame, to take legal proceedings against
Bisland.

I was afraid I would be taken to Stirling jail, discovered,
and taken back to finish my apprenticeship, for by this time
I was as good a tailor as Miller. I therefore left Kippen
and went to Torphichen in Linlithgowshire, where I worked
with a tailor. Hearing that my indenture was lifted, I went

home, and found that my father and mother had started a shop in Charterhall, where they might have made a lot of money had it not been for their family, for, although I was counted the wildest of them, there was one who, under the cloak of religion, was heavier on them than any of us. I was again sent to school, my mother not knowing that all the time I had been absent I was working as a tailor.

I was now at the parish school of St Ninian's, where I began Latin; I attended this school through the day, and at night went to one Robert M'Callum for arithmetic, who was a great arithmetician in his way. His system was one hundred years back, and was not mercantile, being all of a puzzling nature. I also went through a system of book-keeping, mensuration, and trigonometry, and considered myself far enough advanced.

During the time I had a number of breaks at the tailor trade, not for love of it, but whenever my father and I had words I went to it. It is bad for a youth to have a *back-door*, and I knew that the tailor trade rendered me independent of my father. I went to Stirling, to a teacher of arithmetic, named M'Dougal, where I found a thorough change in the system: he threw down a number of figures on my slate, and I was quite unable to work them out; the change in the system was a task quite impracticable for me, I gave him a strange look, and began to talk to myself, saying, "six and four are ten," and so on, when the teacher arrested me. I was convinced of the propriety of his method, but foolishly thought he could have little more than appeared, but the further in the deeper, every new rule brought a new affliction.

I made off to Glasgow, having left my teachers without the knowledge of my parents. I joined a journeyman tailors' house of call, then in the Pipe Close, High Street. It was in the heat of the summer's trade. I got a call to a tailor at the Cross, whose name was M'Luckey, I wrought with him some weeks. Another journeyman and I, one Sabbath morning, were taking a walk in Glasgow Green, where we came across a field preacher holding forth to a large audience, while the lining of his hat spoke more for the feelings of his hearers than himself. The sound of the pence, dashing against each other, to a person of feeling, formed a concert of the most harmonious music, although the preacher was but "a lame brother." We stood for some time and listened, when I happened to say that "I could beat him myself." The next day at our work, merely for pastime, one of the men said, addressing me, "You think you could beat the preacher." I said that "I could," not thinking that it would go any further, but on Saturday night, after our work was over, we fell in with some tailors, when the preaching was brought up. I still said that "I could beat him," when it was agreed that it should be tried the next day. I had no black clothes; the other journeyman went to the "cork" (master) and asked him for the loan of his black suit, pretending that it was for the purpose of attending a funeral.

The next day about 40 of the principal journeymen tailors assembled in the house of call, when I was dressed in the blacks in order to try my "say" in the new profession. I insisted against going to the Green, lest any person from Stirling coming forward might know me. We arranged to go to Westmuir, on the road leading to Airdrie.

At about 12 o'clock we set out, about 40 or 50 strong, and by the time we got to Westmuir we had a good congregation. A precentor was selected, "Donald Bell," a journeyman of Mr Lockhart's, a tailor above the "King's Arms," in the Trongate. My father and mother were Burghers, and possessed the works of Ralph Erskine of Dunfermline, whose sermons my mother took great pleasure in reading and hearing read. I had often to read them aloud to her, which although to her a pleasure, was to me a punishment; and, having a good memory, which was much improved at school, I preached one of Ralph Erskine's sermons. I took for my text St John xiii. 7. "What I do thou knowest not now, but thou shalt know hereafter." I pleased the congregation well, and no thanks to me, for Erskine has handled the subject well.

I had got a number of lessons in elocution, for which I had a peculiar liking, and, my voice at that time not being broken, I made a favourable impression on the people. We had an elder chosen to go round with the "hat," but the "dust" (money) came in so quick that there was no need for that.

At the conclusion I thanked them for their kindness, letting them know that I was sent by the Haldane Society on an itinerating mission to the West of Scotland, with little more to depend on than the generosity of the Christian public, when a lash of more "blunt" (money) was pitched into the hat.

We then came to Camlachie, where we counted the collection : it amounted to 13s. and some odds; that night we spent every "ring."

Next Sabbath there was another sermon planned, but I preferred to go to Stewarton, in Ayrshire, where I wrought till the end of harvest.

I was engaged by three farmers at a place called Bloack to keep a school all winter; none were to be admitted but the children of the three farmers and their cottars. I was boarded in one of the houses at 10s. a-week; I behaved exemplarily, and, carefully studying the nature of my scholars, they made rapid advance.

I returned to Glasgow, and began the tailor trade again, and remained at it for nearly two years, but doing no good. Always when I was in trouble I went home, and when I left home, they got no further word from me till I turned up again. At one of my retreats about five miles from home, I engaged to keep a school at a coal work, at a place called Planemure. They had stoned a number of teachers out of the place before I went; my chance was dull, but I undertook it, and found it the hardest task I had ever met. There were only three persons in the whole work who knew their letters; however, with a mixture of patience and diligence, I succeeded beyond expectation; in six months I had a class of 30 reading the Testament, and during that time I never needed to lift a hand. Their former teachers used physical power over their scholars, and it was not likely that the collier, come to the length of manhood, would take one stroke without giving another. However, I worked on other principles, and for English and arithmetic I would put them on a par with any school in Scotland.

After this I began to go fairly to the bad, as, although the mischief was in me, I had never lost conceit of myself till I went with a company of strolling play-actors. After leaving them I went to Edinburgh and fell in with a toy-maker, with whom I agreed to go to England, which I did, and learned that branch of business.

I engaged a hawker, and commenced toy-manufacturing myself; this was a laborious task, and what made it worse was, that my hawker was a very drunken woman, and I could get no account of her sales; I had never before had such an experience, it was soon enough, however, and I am now particularly well acquainted with such cattle. I held on with her as long as I could, till she would give me neither count nor reckoning.

As yet, I was not a practical drunkard, and had no regard for drink, except when in company; but the scene is now changed, and women have done it.

Dropping the toys, and parting with the "blower," I entered myself apprentice to a china mender, with whom I travelled the country for nine months. This is an excellent travelling trade to a person who can do the work. After I parted with my master, I began business for myself; I required a hawker, and fell in with another woman; she was an excellent hawker, and got plenty of work, but after it was finished, she forgot to take it home, which put me in perpetual danger. At last her conduct compelled me to leave both her and the china trade.

I then started for Newcastle, and began field-preaching; this was a lucrative job among so many colliers, who were all Methodists; I got so dexterous at that craft, that I might have had a church, and was offered to be admitted into the brotherhood, but was afraid that the "*holes of my robe would not hold a button, and a small breeze of wind would expose the inside work.*" I dropped the preaching and left Newcastle, setting out for Carlisle, where I remained till my money was done. I then started for Scotland, and came into Annandale where I first asked what none owed me, that was "charity," my first "cadge" was in the village of Ecclefechan in Dumfriesshire.

After this I attempted at different times and by different means, to work a passage through the world, but partly through the want of good resolution, or from simplicity, I always failed; I have only this for comfort, I never by any means wronged mankind of one penny; although they are yet alive who have wronged me out of thousands. When I arrived at the age of thirty, having come through vicissitudes and miseries that the world never did, nor shall hear of, and seeing no possibility of ever redeeming myself, I then let slip the spirit, that till then I had preserved, and faced a stormy world with a company of wanderers, whose professions were below the dignity of manhood, and whose conditions were below the level of common beggars.

I remained only a short time in this society, we held our way to the Fife coast; the first stop that we made was at Kincardine, where we turned our pence into half-pence. The next night we stayed at Toryburn, which place we left without paying our way, and entered Dunfermline, fourteen in number, without one half-penny in the company. Here was the first bare-faced imposition that ever I saw practiced. We asked for lodgings, and found a respectable widow woman who was in the habit of keeping lodgers. She let two rooms. After a little arrangement, they asked her to boil the kettle, which was done, and brought to the room, the table was covered with a cloth and china, but with no food on it. The company then struck up a conversation as if they were feasting like princes, and had retinues of servants at command.

We posted bills, after securing a house to perform in, but got no encouragement, and after a night's work, our rewards were one-and-twopence "the piece." Each of us tried at how little expense we could fill an empty belly; we stayed there next night also, but making things no better, we divided. A party went to Inverkeithing, where what they drew scarcely paid the lights and the house. I then disengaged myself from the party, crossed the Firth at Queensferry, and went to Edinburgh.

CHAPTER II.

STARTING ON "THE ROAD."—1815.

ECCLEFECHAN in Dumfriesshire was the first place I begged in. At the first door I went to, the woman gave me a piece of bread; and at the next, the wife made me a " blaw " (meal) bag, of which I was muckle the better, and so started briskly on the cadge. After cadging the village and going to the "padden-ken" (lodging house), I meted my meal and found that I had eight tankards, that stands for a jigger's peck, it would sell at 3d., this with 5d. in coppers, and plenty of bread and cheese, was my first day's cadge. The keeper of the lodging-house was " radge " (half crazy), and I had one of the funniest nights I ever passed in my life. Next day I travelled to Langholm, and took up my abode in a house which kept nine " snouses " (rough beds). They were all filled, and with difficultly I got in, on condition that I would snooze on the floor. My companions were sweeps, " cairds," roughs, common cadgers, and " high flyers." The town in ordinary times was worth, between meal and money, from three to four shillings, besides "panem" (bread), and beef.

After that I travelled by Hawick and Jedburgh, calling at every town on that south boundary of Scotland, till I reached Berwick; the town was not good, owing to a man of the name of Barney Duthie, who was detected with his wife, daughters, and servant, and tried for forging " shans " (issuing false coin). The whole five were under the sentence of death. On that account I had to cross the brig and stop in Tweedmouth. Here I met a corps of " routers " (real or pretended wives or widows of soldiers or sailors), on their road from London to Aberdeen. I had a night's fuddle with them, when they turned out as many schedules of marriage, discharges of their husbands, and passes of routes, as might set up a speech-crier. There were nine of them—Highland and Irish. They had an Edinburgh Almanac to help them to find out officers' names in the different regiments.

They engaged me to travel with them to Aberdeen. I got a pound note of "arles" (engagement fee), and I confess them to be the greatest sharpers and imposters I have ever met in the course of my twenty years' travel. We started next morning by Eyemouth to Ayton, having their "routes" relieved in both parishes, and in gentlemen's houses on the road. They received two "screeve" (pounds).

When we were in Cowdenham (Coldingham) Muir, we were passed by the 42nd Regiment, who had landed at Sunderland, on their return from Waterloo (1815).

As soon as we arrived at Dunbar the schedules of routes were filled up, stating that their husbands belonged to the 42nd Regiment, and had fallen at Waterloo. We then divided, the one party going by Stirling and Perth, the other passing through Fife. We met at Dundee, and the parties from Edinburgh had, of clear cash, 27 "screeve" (£27). We then started north in two divisions, the one holding by Coupar-Angus, Forfar, and Brechin, to meet the other party by Arbroath and Montrose. After arranging their routes, I went with the Arbroath party.

On my way between Johnshaven and Bervie, I met with a traveller, who told me that he had met with five women and three children in the hands of some constables, who had been detected at a gentleman's house with false "routes," and were being taken to Stonehaven jail. I then made a stand; I durst not go forward, lest they would "snitch" me, and if I went back the way I had come, I was afraid of pursuit.

I crossed the country to Laurencekirk, and met the other party to whom I communicated the "pulling match." We then went to Blairgowrie stopping at Lochee, and next day crossed to Broughty Ferry, and landed at Portencraigs. As this was the party that went by Stirling they were not known in Fife. We went by Cupar, crossing Fife to Queensferry, and at the south ferry each took their own road. I took one of them in company, and travelled for England, we entered Brampton in Cumberland ; the woman with me was a bred tinker, and could turn her hand to anything in travelling.

She started the southering (soldering), it took well in that country, and some days we could make 20s.; we travelled together till we reached Manchester, where we fell in with another corps of "routers," on their way to Galway in Ireland; she had travelled with them before, and wished to do so again; she proposed it to me in an anxious manner, but I told them I would never join such a gang; they then wished me to fill up their schedules, but I was aware of their treachery, and would not do so.

The next morning she started with them for Liverpool and left me "skirling" for my loss.

I then went to Leeds and stayed some time in Yorkshire; this is the land of the cadger; it is the most charitable county in the three kingdoms, if not in the world. I estimate the number of vagrants in Yorkshire at 15,000, and the expense of their support, taking them by the lump at £25 a-year, would break the contractor in nine months.

On a common near Leeds I met with the first camp of real gipsies I ever saw. They are a courteous and hospitable people; they called me into a tent, and set a lunch before me that the first nobleman in England might have feasted on. I joined the camp and continued with them about four months. It was then near the end of October, and they were retiring to towns for winter quarters. There were about seventy of them, old and young. We flitted three times during my stay; I left them in the county of Lincoln, came down to the north, and wintered in Newcastle-on-Tyne. I fell in after that with different camps of gipsies, and on account of knowing their "cant" (special "slang" language), found an easy access to their friendship. They keep all strangers out of their secrets; I never saw their sovereign who, at that time I understood, was an old man in an encampment in Devonshire.

The gipsies are scrupulous of strangers, trusty in friendship but do not contract them, and in spite revengeful, even to the murder of their relations. They are not idlers, and I never knew any of them begging in the camp. The men work at all kinds of tin-ware and plaiting. They can make moulds for any coin with exactness, and I have seen them cast "shans" (false coin), that would stand three months. They are excellent at fancy work, and the women the most acute fortune tellers, and ring and trinket droppers, that ever I witnessed.

On my return to Edinburgh I shifted from Bell's Wynd to the Canongate, and took my quarters at the house of John Brown, a shoemaker. This man kept a room with three beds in it. In one of the beds lay two boot closers, pupils of Brown's ; I had another, and the remaining one was occupied by one William Skeldon and his family, he, his wife, a daughter about twenty-four, and a boy about fourteen occupying it.

Skeldon, who was a native of Clackmannanshire, told me that he was bred a mason in Alloa, but, if ever he was a mason, the houses he helped to build would make a very small town. He was in the habit of sitting as a beggar on the roads round Edinburgh, with his hands drawn up, as if they were powerless, and the givers of charity, had to put the money into his pocket. He and the wife got drunk every night, and, when they cast out, the hands that were amissing through the day, had to defend him at night.

It was in summer, and I have often seen Skeldon start about three o'clock in the morning, and go to the different roads round, where he lay down and begged, pretending that he had to be out all night, for want of money to pay his bed ; and I have often seen him return between eight and nine in the morning with plenty of money and loaded with food. Skeldon's begging at that time was worth, on an average, 6s. or 7s. a-day.

His daughter was a good-looking woman, and had three professions which she daily followed, a strumpet, a shoplifter, and a pickpocket. When she went out she dressed in style, sometimes without a shirt. One day, I was selling books in the Flesh Market, and saw her there; a lady had got her pocket picked, and there was a crowd round her ; on my return to the house I found Katy ; her father and mother were out drinking, and I saw a purse half burnt in the grate, which a young girl told me Katy had taken a handful of gold and silver out of, and I suspected it belonged to the lady. One night, Katy was in company with some young gentlemen, one of whom she " skinned " of three five-pound notes; she was charged with the theft, ran off, but, at Brown's door, was seized by a policeman, and taken to the Canongate office.   On being searched nothing was found on her; and she was dismissed.

After her liberation the notes turned up; on finding the first she opened it out, dried it at the fire, and invited us all out to get a dram.   She went to a cellar kept by a man named Peck, to whom she presented the note for change; on looking at it he made some "very unsavoury" remarks, but gave her four pound notes, and a pound in silver for it.

Sometimes I tried the "pad" (begging) on the roads round Edinburgh.   The Canonmill's Road, as a "pad," when I first started, was worth on an average, about 5s. and a few "browns" (pence), daily.   The Bonnington Road was pestered with pads, sometimes to the amount of ten and twelve. From Broughton Road to Newhaven, from ten in the morning till six at night, was worth from 1s. 6d. to 2s..

The King's Park to Piershill Barracks was not worth anything except on Sunday.   When I first begged on it with my hat in my hand, the first Sunday, from three till nine o'clock, I was worth 17s. and some pence, but before I left the city, there was such a number there, and their conduct was so bad, that one half could "turn" it any day.

I was back and forward in Edinburgh at least nine years, and only once in the police office.   That was for calling books with a mob round me in Hanover Street, for which I got a severe reprimand.   I left "Auld Reekie" and took the Road to Glasgow.

The first night I halted at Broxburn, and stayed in a lodging kept by a tailor.   There were two different clans of tinkers lodging there; after disputing their qualifications as budget bearers, they started the subject of religion—the one party was called Ryllie, and declared themselves Roman Catholics—the other, of the name of Cochran, calling themselves Protestants.   The argument was ably debated on both sides, the words were few, but the arguments were good.

The precise part which each speaker addressed was the "knowledge box" of his antagonist, and the "*language*" used was that of soldering irons and tongs.   At last one of the Cochran's received a blow which left his eye on his cheek; this made him roar up and down the house like a "banshee" (an Irish fairy).   His wife, who was plying a noble fist with a poker, and at every stroke was saying "suther (solder) yet," got her eye on her husband, in his distress about his "glim" (eye), when she, with the poker, made a slap at the other eye, saying, "is it your eye you are making a work about?" and thus winning the battle.

I then started for Airdrie, it is a good town for selling a book; here I sent to Glasgow, and got some quires of "Janet Clinker's Orations," when I alarmed Airdrie for the first time with my street lectures. I stayed there a week, and through the day went through the collier towns collecting "the poor rates." The colliers are good for meal, but, never look to them for half-pence, except on pay day. I then went to Hamilton by Bellshill, this is a poor village for a cadger; one half is in poverty, and the other half not willing. I did not get two tankards of meal in the village.

Next morning I went to Dalziel; this village turned out near a peck of meal and some coppers. I went to a gentleman's house on the east of the village; as I went up the avenue I met an old gentleman, and begged from him; he asked me if I had anything to shew (he meant a pass.) I said "No."

As I spoke, a cadger on the look-out for house-breaking, with a respectful bow, handed him a "chat" (certificate.) The gentleman read it, and asked the man what he wanted. He said "Charity."

The gentleman gave him a strange look, and holding up the "chat" said, "charity with that? That could get you in to be an elder in any parish church. Were I asking a character, the person who would give me such a character would be a greater rascal than myself." And reaching me half-a-crown, said: "You, without the character, and I believe can get one, take that; but you *decent* man with the character, I have nothing that I can spare you." We both came down the avenue together, and the "high-flyer" said that he was a burglar.

I went that night to Hamilton, this is a town that is very hard, but I called it with "Watty and Meg," telling them that "it was a cure for ill wives," and I suppose the men *knew* that they needed it. On the Saturday night, I drew upwards of 7s. On Monday I went to Laverockhall. (Larkhall.) This is a charitable village, and in it and the neighbourhood, I made ten tankards of meal, and some bread.

Next day I went to Stonehouse, and made 1s. 1d.; I then went to Glasgow, without calling Kilbride, on account of the poor character that it got among travellers.

When I got to Glasgow I took lodgings in Lady Marshall's Close, in the Bridgegate, where I lodged with an Irishman, a stone-mason; he kept three beds. I occupied one, the other two were occupied by boys. Next morning I asked the landlady what these boys did? she said " they sold articles about the town," but I soon found out that the wares they carried were first " *found* " and then sold.

There were always from four to six of them; they were dexterous in their profession. One of them named Robert Wilson (whose father was a horrid character, and kept a low public-house in the High Street), always attended when there was a crowd. This boy was always consulted when they wanted to know what fairs were coming on, and he would look the almanack, and let them know.

One of these boys was a poor innocent; he was Irish, had straggled from home, and came to Glasgow; for some time after he came, he sang ballads in the streets; he afterwards dropped singing, and joined the band. He was soon well-dressed, and made a good offer at the trade. I often observed him, and saw signs of remorse in his countenance.

One day one of the Wilson's told him he was going to Paisley to be a " drawboy " to a weaver, and was going to leave them; poor James Kenney gave him a look of pity, saying. " Go back, and seek God to guide you, and be thankful that you can ' draw.' I would be thankful if I could, but I can do nothing but sing, and steal, and I will be hanged yet; and, bursting into tears, he went to the door, crying."

After this unfortunate boy had remained for some eighteen months in this gang, his mother, a poor old woman, came from Belfast and took him home. The woman that kept the lodging house, a notorious character, went to Belfast and brought him back. The last I heard of him, was, that at Ayr, he was transported for fourteen years.

CHAPTER III.

THE DENS OF GLASGOW.

I THEN left Lady Marshall's Close, and came to the foot of the Old Wynd, and took lodgings in a celebrated spot, called the "Flea Barracks." This place was on a ground floor, near a dung heap. It was kept by an Irish woman. I heard her tell that when she came to Glasgow she had only 1s. 2½d., with the shilling she took the house in the "Flea Barracks," with the 2½d. she purchased coals, and made a fire.

She then stood at the door, and, as the unfortunate women passed and repassed, she said to them, "that they might come in, if they got a chance;" as they called, she gave them the length and breadth of the floor. She sold them whisky, which she had purchased at the cheapest rate, for 6d. a gill; and by five o'clock in the morning, she was possessed of 6s. 6d.

One of these women was good looking, clever at soldering, and a fortune-teller. Every night the room was full of lasses getting their fortunes told at 3d. each. She could contract her tongue and show as if she wanted it; and could draw her ear in such a manner that it appeared to be entirely shut.

The landlady was a passer of false coins, and, besides her business in the town, she went to all country fairs. She had a daughter who was as good at passing counterfeit coin as herself. It was the daughter's duty every morning to go about the street looking for a sour (butter) milk cart, and a simple looking person along with it; she would purchase milk and butter, passing the bad money, in this manner did this notorious person bring up her family.

One of her sons received sentence of death at Glasgow. At this time George the Fourth, was in Ireland; the mother set out to Ireland to intercede with the King for her son's life; but, finding no opportunity of getting an interview, she, when the King was leaving to return to England, as he went on board the vessel, threw herself into the water, which raised a commotion, and attracted the attention of the King. When he understood that she did this because she could not gain an audience with him, he commanded her to be brought before him; and, on hearing the reason of her rash attempt, let her understand that he would pardon her son, which he did; and her son was transported to Australia.

He carried along with him the bad principles which he had inherited from his parents. He deserted three times; for the first two offences he received three years' hard labour underground, the third time he escaped. He had many hair-breadth escapes, and, on reaching Glasgow sought the Old Wynd; but by this time his mother and the family had gone to America, and his connections, fearing the worst from such a character, sent him out to his parents in New York. The "Flea Barracks," to my knowledge, have been the resort of all sorts of bad characters for the last thirty years.

I removed to Gorbals, to the house of a woman named Mary Gillespie, who kept a lodging-house of 13 beds, which were full every night, besides two beds which she kept for those who could not pay. This woman was the most charitable person I have ever met with in all my travels.

At this time petty house thefts were taking place every day, and, when a theft was committed they had recourse to a devilish proceeding, namely, turning the key on a verse of the Bible, and whoever the key lights against is held guilty; but I do not intend to go through the process, as it would be laying down principles for the corruption of morality, which would be contrary to the intention of this publication, Another man and I remonstrated against turning the key, at the same time threatening to cause the landlady trouble, and the system was dropped.

A pair of blankets was stolen from one of the beds, which

caused a great stir in the house; they would have tried the key, but were afraid to do so. It was necessary to find the thief, and they took the oath of all the house; this was done by the woman of the house taking an oath on a book, and handing round the book to all in the house; and whoever would not take the oath was considered guilty. The person before mentioned and myself would not take the oath, and we were considered guilty by all in the house except the landlady, who knew us; we took the odium very calmly. But justice is not always under a cloud. About two months after, the wife of a vagrant who had removed to Paisley, and there was struck with remorse of conscience, sent her husband back with the pawn ticket of the blankets that she had stolen and pledged. That showed the meanness of the man, to undertake such a task to cover a thief, as he knew his wife to be.

I removed again to the Old Wynd, and lodged in the Highland Close, with an old "reprobate" of an Irishwoman, who came from Ireland accompanied by a blind cadger, by whom she had a son; he left her, took another woman and started a disreputable house in Allison's Close, Edinburgh.

The woman with whom I resided in the Old Wynd had 3s. 6d. from the "Session" (church funds for paupers); she sent to Ireland for her mother, who was getting off the "Session" also; there was another lodging-house on the ground floor, where lived five lodgers, all of whom were getting money from the "Session."

The "Session" day came round, and my landlady went and drew 7s. for her mother and herself; when she returned she gave her mother half-an-ounce of tobacco, saying, "that is your share of the Session money," she went out, and when she returned half drunk, she was accompanied by a young Irishman about 18 years of age; they went in and out for some time, and ultimately he came in carrying the woman in his arms; she was put to bed, and on her mother searching her, she found no money. In this way the greater part of "Session" money goes.

In the flat below lived another Irishwoman, who was also receiving money from the Session; she went about with a bottle of whisky which she bartered with weavers for weft (yarn used for woof), and in this way made a better livelihood than by honest industry, yet she was not satisfied; she had the Irish nature, and greed is never satisfied. She determined to get something more from the " Session," although, when she was last there, she was told not to come back, and " CHEEK " being the *muckle part* of beggary, she obtained a powder with which she painted every part of her body which was uncovered, and with two neighbours, one supporting each arm, she set out for the " Session."

I looked out of the window after them, and saw every person looking at her, imagining that she was going to the Infirmary, such a shocking appearance did she present. I was sure she would succeed in getting more money from the "Session," as they would consider that the next charge on them would be the expense of a coffin for her. She received 2s. 6d., and, when the three came home, the festival began.

An old man was in the house, by tongue a Highlander and by dress a sailor. As the drink went round he got his share; and, as she tasted, the woman who had such a dying appearance began to revive, and at last she swore that when she was a girl of 14, there was not a girl round Machara who could dance Jack-o'-Tar with her. I was in the room above, and applying my eye to the board, could see all below. She lifted the jacket and trousers of the sailor. A woman took the poker and tongs, and sang and "played the fiddle," while the woman danced. Had any of the Session seen them, they would hardly have considered that their 2s. 6d. was well laid out.

While lodging in the Saltmarket, there was a wretched mother and her four children in the house. Their name was M'Leish; the mother was in the habit of sending her children out to beg and steal. One night the children came in at ten o'clock, and they had not as much as pleased the mother, who was drunk; with a volley of oaths she ordered them out to find more; the children had, no doubt, done their best, but that would not do—she wanted more drink, and the price of the lodgings,—and, looking to the oldest, a girl about 18 years old, said she " would make her go out and find it," adding that "she might get it in a short time from a gentleman."

The girl cried, and said, " You took me from the cotton

mill and forced me to beg and steal, and now you will compel me to ruin soul and body for nothing but to support your drunken habits." On hearing this, the landlord made the children sit down, and told the mother that it was only on account of the lateness of the hour that he did not put her out of the door. If those who keep lodgings would act in this manner it would be well for society.

During my stay here, one Sabbath, after the two o'clock bells had rung, I was standing in the doorway, when a woman came down the Wynd with something rolled up in her apron. When she came up to me she halted, and showed me a sheep's head, half boiled, with some barley sticking on it; she asked me if "I would buy it?" I asked what she wanted for it? She said her husband had given 5d. for it, and a penny for "singeing" it. I said, "it was nothing to me what her husband paid for it, but what was she asking for it?" She said 3d., as "that sum would get her a glass."

I gave her the money; she went to the Goosedubs and drank the money. As she passed me on returning, I said, "when your husband misses the sheep's head, you will get a terrible licking, and, if he should happen to kill you, will it not be a pity to see a man hanged for such a drunken drab as you are?" She said, "she would get a licking, but she could not help it now." I told her, "if she would put the head back in the pot, I would give it to her." She promised, and I gave her the sheep's head, but, instead of returning it to the pot, she went and sold it for *a penny*, and went and drank it.

During one of the Fair days of Glasgow, the landlady and I were standing in the doorway. She kept a small broker's shop, and had a mantle hanging at the door; an old man came in and priced the mantle; the landlady asked 3s. 6d. An unfortunate woman, who was sitting in the stair opposite, heard her ask 3s. 6d.; she started up, and caught the old man by the arm, saying to the landlady, "Where's your conscience to seek that from an old man for that mantle? Come with me, and I will show you one worth two of it, for half-a-crown."

The old man went with her, and they had scarce time to be in, when we heard him crying "murder;" his hat was cast down the stair, and he after it.   He told us he had 13s. on him, and they had stolen it.   We advised him to go for a policeman; and, when the policeman came to the foot of the stairs, he asked him, " if it was there he was looking for a cloak?   You old rascal, a grave would be liker you," and seizing him by the neck, said, " You shall go with me to the police office."   The old man begged him not to take him there.   The policeman took him to the foot of the Wynd, calling him anything but a decent man, and put him down the Bridgegate.

I next removed to Jamphrie's Close in " the Goosedubs," this place may be called "Beggar Square."   I "pinched" (hardly) think, that there was a Scotch family in it; the whole of the inhabitants of this close, with a few exceptions, exist by begging, keeping lodgings, or some low dealing business, such as " sour dook " (butter milk) cadgers, whelk, mussel, or dulse hawkers, herring or fish droppers, with a number of Irish women, not bred to work, and too lazy to beg; manufacturing sheep's trotters, with their goods in an old basket, sitting from morning to night, or lying over the gutter, with faces that never knew shame.

This part of the town is the Irish quarter, and in many respects they are a much better class than the other two nations; their principles are more noble, and their feelings more charitable.   I mean the poor Irish; I think it is partly on account of their having been in subordination for so many hundred years, subject to a country foreign to them, and strangers to their manners and customs, that disregarded Ireland and its interests, any further than to keep it in subjection.

CHAPTER IV.

THE IRISH "QUESTION."

IRELAND, merely by way of a farce, had a Parliament, but it was bestowed upon them, as a doll is bestowed by a mother upon her child, to divert it from "fashing" (troubling) her. Let any person read the history of the Irish Parliament, from the time that it was first opened under the English Government, till its close in 1800. Led by emissaries under the kings and governments of England—paid for their villanies—intruders on the country—and enemies of its welfare.

Under the existence of such a mock government, the oppressor's part was to do their worst, while the part of the oppressed was to endure such treatment as they received, as best they could, for the long period of 600 years. During that time their land was drenched in blood. The conspiracy, planned in England, and put in execution by unprincipled incendiaries in cases of robbery or murder, if not justified, was at least winked at. These incendiaries, for their "trouble" of persecution, were rewarded by estates of the highest value, and property, the prime of that country.

The poor, who had been so, were doomed, generation after generation, to wallow in their misery. The consciences of such landholders telling them that they could look for no fidelity from the peasantry, not only from the nature of their intrusion on the rights of mankind, but from the manner in which they had slighted the soil and treated the inhabitants.

Estates in Ireland worth from £20,000 to £30,000 a year can be found, in more places than one, where the landlord lives to an old age, and dies without living one year on the property. The time is spent in racking and beggaring the tenants, who from their poverty are unable to cultivate, and the cottars who have no implements, to till the soil. This

sank their spirits, from the fire-bravery which is to be found
in those hardy sons and daughters who were schooled in the
principles of economy.

The thing which has ruined the low class of the Irish in
Scotland is their poverty. When they enter the country,
they usually have large families, for whom they have to take
lodgings; and, sometimes, long before they find employment
they are compelled to take dishonest or downward steps to
support existence. If they enter the lodgings innocent, they
receive examples of roguery which soon corrupt their morals.
The houses in which they live contain one or two apartments,
and are let by the week, the rent of which must be paid
beforehand.

This system looks as if it were made for the good of the
poor, but it must be viewed in another light; by the rapid
emigration of families, settling in large towns where public
works and commerce are engaged in, the landlords take
advantage of this to raise the rents to extortion, of houses
which should have been taken down to the ground long ago;
which are utterly uninhabitable, and which give rise to
noxious diseases not only to the inmates of the houses, but,
like plagues, spread over the whole neighbourhood.

The wretchedness of the houses infect the women, who in
general are bred in miry places, and never know what clean-
ing a house is. They are never pushed to emulate their
neighbours in cleanliness, every article in the house being
covered with dirt. Even their own persons are unclean,
they sit at their fireside from morning to night, with their
lazy companions burning tobacco; and, although the house
be overgrown with dirt, the women never find time to clean
it, whereas, if they were placed, one or two in a neighbourhood, the spirit of emulation would incite them to principles
of housewifely economy.

I now left Glasgow and went to Paisley, here I lodged in
the " Ropery " Close, in the High Street. There are three
" Ropery " Closes, and two in particular have been the seat
of roguery for years; not a house in the " Ropery " but
is filled with cadgers, depending mostly on misplaced charity;
and on Saturdays, a cunning gambling vagabond may get
from 15s to 18s between halfpence and small silver.

Paisley and a number of villages in the neighbourhood are

excellent ground for the cadger; he may remain in Paisley, and live on the best of the land. From the number of beds in Paisley, Johnstone, Barrhead, and Neilston, that each lodging-house keeps, I cannot estimate under 150 vagrants daily; making allowance for numbers of them who reside with friends, and have houses of their own. Allow each of them 1s. a day on an average, which some will not make, but where *one* falls short, *three* will go far beyond that sum, aye, double the shilling, which makes a heavy tax on Paisley. On a fair investigation of every 200, you will not find forty objects of charity. From this let Paisley balance and see how many real objects of charity might be supported in an ordinary way on this sum.

In Paisley a "keelie" (street arab) is ill to judge, as there are very few "drawboys" that do not know the ways of vagrancy; God forbid that I should say all "drawboys" are thieves, but, as I have said, "cant" (the thieves' language) has been introduced among the "drawboys" of Paisley by disorderly persons entering that department of the weaver's profession, and instilling into them that abominable gabble. This may be accounted for from the poverty of the parents, who hurry their children out to bring in money, and their education is thus neglected.

I lodged in the School Wynd with a man named Coriston, who possessed two apartments, but only one fireplace. I have seen as many as forty lodgers in the house at one time, from whom he got 3d a head, if they were above fifteen. The greater part of them were not travellers, but Irish women, whose husbands were lurkers about or were working in the town. Some of them had two or three children in the public works, while the wife and the younger children were every day on the "cadge." One of these families went to the chapel on Sundays with clothes as respectable as any ordinary family in Paisley. One Sabbath day the husband counted their week's income. It amounted to £1 13s. besides the wife's cadge, which he allowed to keep them in meal and tobacco.

Some years after that, I was crying down Moss Street, and took a notion of a glass of whisky. I went into a shop, and, as I was taking it, I looked at the face at the back of the counter, but at the time could not recollect where I had seen it. After I was in the street I recollected the cadger, who was in Coriston's; I went back to make sure, and said "I thought I had seen her before." She answered, "It is possible." When I looked at their rise and their present splendour, in the very place where people knew they were beggars, and their conscience told them they had imposed on the public. I then considered that I, in the street with a halfpenny paper in my hand, was a better man than they in the shop.

During my stay in Coriston's, one night, after potato lifting, a Connaught man came to the door and asked lodgings, but said that he could not pay, as he had been robbed coming from the harvest, and had been two days without food. Coriston told him that no one would get lodgings there who had no money. A few lodgers round the fire made up the price of his bed and supper; next morning they collected for his breakfast and tobacco, and he went off.

After breakfast I went to the room to look over a paper I had got the night before; a woman was making the beds, and found, in the one in which the man had lain, a pocket-book, which she showed to me; on opening it we found that it contained £3 12s., and we concluded that it was the Irish-man's, as none had lain in the bed but him.

The woman asked me "if she would give it to Coriston?" I said "Coriston had no right to it, as he would not be one halfpenny at the collection, that there was no fear but that the man would be back for it; and if he did not come at night, I would give it to those who had collected for him, and leave it to their judgment, whether he should return the money they had collected for him," when she agreed that I should keep it.

Shortly after, a girl came in requesting me to go to Mr Neilson's printing office, about an eight-page book that George Caldwell, senior, was getting printed for me. I went, and while I was away, which would be about two hours, the man returned, and said he "had forgotten something which he had left in the bed." The landlady asked him "what it was? as the bed was made, and they had seen nothing." On hearing this Pat roared out, "Murder, and robbery."

Coriston, who was cat-witted at the best, asked him "where he was robbed, and what he had been robbed of?"

He said "he had been robbed of his harvest money." Coriston said "he had told that yestr'een, and what was the use of roaring about it now?" The Irishman roared, "I had £3 12s. when I came into your unlucky house, and went to your unlucky bed." Coriston got into a passion, took a stick, turned Paddy out at the door, and Paddy bolted down the School Wynd, Coriston following.

The Police Office was then at the "Cross," and one Richardson, a policeman, passing up Moss Street, took them both into the office. When I returned they told me the story. The woman who had found the book gave me a meaning look. I was in a "habble" (scrape); I had the money and the book, and there was danger in keeping them. The woman followed me out of the place, and asked me "what I was going to do?" I told her "I did not know;" she asked me if I would give her the half of it. I handed her the book with the whole, and she went off.

Coriston was bailed out, and the Irishman was kept till next day, when the whole house was called, and corroborated each other's evidence; how the Irishman came to the house, what he stated, and what the lodgers had done for him. The magistrate asked him "if he objected to the evidence?" He admitted its truth, but maintained that he had lost the money. The magistrate considered Paddy an impostor, as he was, and sent him out of the town with a policeman, telling him that it was a pity "Bridewell" was not finished.

Paisley was the first town that ever I imposed on, by selling useless paper for books. One Saturday night I could get no books to buy, as there was only one bookseller in Paisley who sold them, George Caldwell, residing in Dyer's Wynd, Moss Street, who had retired from business; and in a room of his dwelling-house was selling off the remainder of his stock.

That night he was out, and had taken the key of the room along with him; I wearied waiting for him, and seeing a number of papers lying on the kitchen table, I bargained for them with Mrs Caldwell; and she, honest woman, not knowing the purpose for which I wanted them, sold them to me. I went out into the street, told a long tale, and sold the papers. Times were good then; I drew upwards of 4s. None challenged me that night, but on the Monday following when I was at the "Cross," a young woman came to me and said, "You rascal, you cheated me on Saturday night; you sold me a newspaper instead of a book." I asked her "What she gave for it?" She said, "A halfpenny." And I told her she "could never be cheated with a newspaper for a half-penny."

I left Paisley, and determined to go to England. I only got to Whitby, in Yorkshire, when I was compelled to turn. At that time the builders in Edinburgh made a stop, which cast thousands of people over the country in starvation; they were all over England, and the most of them being acquainted with me, I scarcely could enter a lodging but I met some of them in distress. I could not sit down to meat and see them fasting; neither could I find support for them. At that time there was never a sturdy beggar, tinker, or lurker, but was through England with aprons before them pretending to be masons, wrights, or plasterers, "girning" (crying out) about the dulness of trade, and receiving money in pocketfuls; each of them with a dandy of a beggar's "shakedown," sitting in the lodging-house like ladies of honour till the impostors would come in with the purse.

In this excursion I have seen masons and wrights coming to the lodging-houses begging for a night's lodgings without a morsel of supper or breakfast; while the low beggars, taking advantage of their distress, and making money "like slate-stanes," never offered these unfortunate, real tradesmen a morsel of food. I was sorry to see the public so ignorantly blind, to think that it was doing charity to put their money in the hands of impostors; or did they think that a respect-able tradesman would bemean himself to sing on the street? I have known them, by strong necessity, make known their wants to a fellow-creature, but to *sing* on the street requires a person who is a stranger to shame.

CHAPTER V.

A BIRTHRIGHT FOR A MESS OF POTTAGE.

DURING my trip in England an uncle of mine died in Stirlingshire, of whom I was heir-at-law, but on account of my rambling disposition he became my mortal enemy. When he was old he married a woman in order to have an heir of his own, but she had no children, and died some years before him. The woman was an economist, and behaved with great prudence in every respect, particularly towards him; whether during her life he made over all to her I never knew, but as the wife turned frail, she got a niece to superintend the house, which was a piece of home-bred economy for which I have no grudge against her, but after her death the niece got the " lee-side " of the doating old man, and, with some other of her friends, got him to make a will in their favour.

The will was made within a few days of his death, and on the bed from which he never rose; it settled on his wife's niece all his property, both houses and household furniture, with £300 to two nephews of the wife, £30 to two more who were too rich already and not one drop of blood either to him or the wife, and to whom perhaps he never spoke twenty times in his life; he also bequeathed away the rest of his property to his niece fourteen years younger than I, leaving me £3 at her death, and a paltry sum to a cousin of mine who had an equal right with myself.

Shortly after my return from England, I met a farmer from the place, who informed me that my uncle was dead, and that I should go home, telling me that there was a will made a few days before his death, but it was the opinion of the country that the will was not legal, and advising me to step forward and claim my rights, adding that several friends would come forward to help me.

I was aware of that, and wrote to a gentleman in Stirling, who was intimate with my uncle, and who, I expected, would have been consulted about the settlement of his affairs. I received an answer from him saying that he knew nothing of the settlement, neither was he at the funeral, at the same time forwarding me a power of attorney, authorising him to prosecute on my behalf for a sight of the will. An action was raised by me against the heirs-at-" will " by Mr Boyd, writer in Stirling; the business was transmitted to Edinburgh, and put in the hands of Henry Fotheringham, Writer to the Signet, who raised an action of reduction in the Court of Session.

On receiving the summons, John Rae, Esq. of Milquarter, one of the legatees, came to Edinburgh, and tried to make a settlement with me; he offered me a sum to hand over my rights. My cousin, who had equal right with me, but who was more *religious* than *sensible*, would not come forward and join me in the prosecution. I wrote to him several times, and partly on account of his wife having died and left him with a large family of children under age, and partly that all he was possessed of was lying in a broken bank in Stirling; these things tethered (hampered) his conscience, and he had also promised to his uncle that he would not interfere with the will.

The case came on before the Lords of Council and Session, who, after examination, declared the will null and void, and that William Archibald, the other heir-at-law with myself, having declined to prosecute, had no claim.

People will now think that the old beggar and speech-crier was a rich man, but 'stop ye there!' WHISKY lay between it and me. As soon as the heirs " by will " found they had lost all, they employed two men to take me into a public house and make me drunk.

I was drunk when they fell in with me, and the conquest was easy. I was soon insensible, and in that state, whether by me or another I know not, but my hand was signed to a disposition giving up my right to the whole, and when I awakened there.was £100 in my pocket.

When I understood what I had done I drank the WHOLE

to 1s. 6d., before I suffered myself to be sober or knew what I was doing. When I found out what I had done I left Edinburgh never more to behold it.

I held to the south and stayed at Loanhead, a straggling village seven miles from Edinburgh. I cadged it, and had thirteen tankards of meal. The next day I crossed Soutrahill and landed at Lauder; this is a poor town, and to be envied for nothing but its great quantities of good milk. When I was there I had a sight of Lauderdale Castle, for which I paid 1s. My curiosity led me there, as in that castle were deposited all the instruments of cruelty which were used during the Persecutions, of which I had a good sight. I saw the Scottish "rack," the "thumb finger screws," and two other bits which were used as instruments of cruelty, of which, and a number of other articles, the keeper could give me no account.

I then went to Melrose; this is a small town, but with a number of rich people in it. I could not have made as much as would have paid my bed in this town had it not been for a gentleman from Edinburgh, from whom I received a handsome present.

From Melrose I went to Galashiels. On the Saturday night, a woman was brought in a wheelbarrow to the door of the lodgings where I was staying. The keeper of the lodging-house declined to take her in on account of the disease from which she seemed to be suffering, but I insisted on him taking her in, and she was admitted. When she was wheeled into the room, she asked for a glass of whisky to revive her, which she received; in a little she desired another, which the landlady declined to give.

The woman told the landlady if it was dark she would get it and no thanks to her. When it turned grey she got up, went to her bundle and took out clothes, washed and dressed herself, and soon appeared a trim good-looking woman, and went out. After some hours she returned half drunk with a number of children after her, who little knew she was the woman they had wheeled to the door of the lodgings a few hours before, helpless and diseased.

An Irishman living in the house who made basses considered her a *desirable* woman, and on the Sabbath they made a match of it, only he objected to the barrow. On Monday morning the young couple started for Selkirk. She had " called " it on the Friday in the barrow, and had been sent on to Galashiels. She was struck with blindness this time, but they found her out and sent her to jail, and she got 30 days' confinement.

After cadging Gordon and Greenlaw I went on to Swinton, where I remained a week on account of a Fair which was to take place at Dunse, six miles from Swinton. The country round is rich with fine villages. During my stay in Swinton a woman with a boy that was half crazy came to the lodging-house, and an Irishman came to the house with four pecks of meal and a great cargo of pease bannocks, which is the general bread of that country. The boy asked him if he had " gathered all that that day ; " he said "he had," and turning to his mother the boy said, " That would make a fine man for you, mother," and asked him " if he would take her ; " he said " he would." With that the kettle was put on the fire, and he invited her to drink tea with him, and during the tea the bargain was concluded.

Next day he ordered the young wife to keep the house and he would go out himself, and, turning round at the door, told her " to send the boy through the town to gather potatoes." On hearing that the boy turned round, saying, " Mother, if I must gather potatoes you shall not be his wife another night." With that the young man set out on the cadge.

On that afternoon a cadger pretending blindness came to the house and struck up another match with her. The crazy boy was better pleased, for he told his mother " that this one was blind, and when he got a piece of bread or beef they would eat it and he would not see them." They got supper and went to bed. About an hour after that, the last night's husband came to the door. The landlady refused him admission, saying, that the rooms were full, and his wife had gone.

He might have left the house, but the boy was so much taken up with his new father that he could not hold his peace, and roared out to him, ordering him " to go about his business for an Irish rascal," telling him " his mother had got a man worth ten of him." With that Paddy broke open the door, and the new-made couple prepared for battle ; Paddy never took time to unharness his bags, but, fully accoutred, engaged in a battle which consisted of swearing, tearing, and boxing.

Poor Paddy got no justice, as all three were against him, the boy crying, "Blind daddy, maul the Irish scoundrel." In the heat of the struggle they tumbled over the trap and then went out of doors. The house stood in the square of the town, and they boxed there till the whole folks in the town turned out; who, after witnessing the battle for a while, seized on all three and dragged them to a pump-well, where, after cooling their "clocking," stoned them out of the town. The landlady said that the woman had had fifty-three men with her, and these two made fifty-five.

Leaving Swinton, I started for Coldstream on my way to Wooller Fair. When I reached Wooller every house was full, and there was not accommodation for one-half of those who came to the fair. There were a great number of "*finger-smiths*;" these seldom take lodgings, because their chance is best at night for robbery and assault. I did no good in Wooller, although I had papers with me which never missed a sale before.

Little to the credit of the clergy and magistrates of that place, the most infamous and abominable songs that can be picked from the works of the lowest poets that ever wrote, are the articles which sell in Wooller. There was a man and woman selling these abominable songs, and crowds of both males and females were round them buying fast; and I know, that had they appeared in the streets of Glasgow, if there had been neither policemen nor magistrates within 50 miles, the unfortunate women in the Old Wynd would have stoned them out of the town.

The man and woman sold 17 quires of ballads that day, and their profit would be about £3 7s. This is the Scots quire, containing 94 copies in each quire. I have had the cheek, *when I was drunk,* to sing such songs; but, at my worst, I would not take £5 and sing one of them in the presence of a female; and yet the morality of England, even by dress and looks, among families from whom "refinity" might be looked for, I found in the circle of the profane. It put me in mind of the sonnet of Ralph Erskine, where he observes such profanity in the following strains :—

> " But let one bawdy and blasphemous write,
> The lewd and modest both will take delight,
> The blushing virgin, pleased to see and look,
> Will place these poems next the Prayer-book. "

At this fair there were a number of robberies committed during the night, and at Long Horsely, where we went to afterwards. I cadged this village ; it is a great place for oatmeal, which is made much rounder than the oatmeal of Scotland ; it is not made for baking, but intended for " crowdy," which is a great " beverage," and excels ordinary brose by a hundred degrees. The people of this place are charitable, even the poorest give freely ; I got, from door to door, about seven measures of meal, besides money, bread and beef.

Next day we reached Morpeth. This a large town, the County Town of Northumberland. They have a new jail here, and, during the time of its building, no stout beggar would enter the place, as they are immediately apprehended and sentenced to hard labour, sometimes for three months, and are made to serve the masons as labourers. I then went to Bedlington, six miles from Morpeth. This is a good district, and is a country of Methodists. In Morpeth I drew up an account of a murder which was discovered in a church in Glasgow, and found out by the clergyman's clearing up a case of conscience. A person in the church was conscience-stricken, and confessed a murder which he had committed twenty years before. This paper went like hand-bills, and I took within a few pence of 18s.

I went next to Blyth, where it had a good sale, and I sold it all down the coast till I came to North Shields, having nearly sold it off. I would not go to Newcastle, on account of the speech-criers catching it. I went to Sunderland and got it printed ; and to Houghton-le-Spring, and took the towns back to Newcastle, but the speech-criers had it next day.

I then put the " Misfortunes of Simple John," and the " Gauger's Journey to the Land of Darkness," before the town. I began at one end of Pilgrim Street, and, before I was half-way at the other I had a crowd round me, which, I must confess, was by far too large. The constables carried me off to the *coal-hole,* and next day, I was brought before the magistrates and sentenced to seven days in the House of Correction, and to be put out of the town.

I started on the Morpeth Road, and called at every gentleman's hall, and, before I reached Morpeth, I was loaded like a "cuddy." It came on a hurricane of rain, and I meant to try a change from the place I had stayed in before, which was kept by a sharper. I was directed to the end of the town, next Felton, where was a yard full of lodging-houses. I knocked at the door, but on account of the wind blowing they did not hear me, and I stood at the door some time. While waiting, a woman of about twenty came, and, in the Cockney accent, asked me "If this was a lodging-house?" I said it was. She asked me "If I was a traveller?" I said "I was a kind of one." She then asked, "If I had a wife?" I said, "No." She then asked me "If I would take her for one?" and I said, "I would." With that the door opened. She took the word from me, and asked the landlady "If she had a bed for her and her husband?" She said, "She could," and turned in.

I went in last, and asked, "If she could give me lodgings?" When the Cockney turned round to me and asked, "If the wind had driven me dolt. Did I not hear that I was to get a bed?" With that I took a seat, and in a little after she said, "She wished she had a cup of tea." I thought to myself, "Lady, you think you have got a flat to deal with;" and I gave her no answer.

All this time I thought she had a husband coming forward; she again asked for tea, saying, "She had plenty of bread and corned beef, and it is a pity we cannot have a cup of tea." I then thought, "Let you have a husband or not, if you have the bread and the beef, I will be the trimmings."

After tea she asked to be shown the bed, and she then stripped the child which was with her, and got into bed. She did not lie long till she called to the landlady, "To take the tongs and beat that fellow from the fireside, for it is his fashion at every place he sleeps at, if he can get any person to hold chit-chat with him, he will sit up to two or three in the morning, when she had to complain to strangers."

They observed that the child looked strange at me, and I thought the child, who was not above four years old, might well look strange at me, never having seen me before. But the laughable part of the thing was, the young goodwife started from her bed, came into the kitchen, and with all the seriousness of a clergyman, said, "O, man! O, man! Is your conscience not checking you yet? No wonder the people tell you that your own flesh and blood look strange at you; it was only fifteen months old when you went out as well pleased as ever you were, and never saw the face of either wife or child till now."

A neighbour that was in the house went out, and made the case known; the house filled, and they started on me like so many terriers. I thought I would have been torn to pieces; I slipped to bed as calm as a mouse. I had a small trifle, which I secured the most of, and, after I was in bed, she showed the woman what she had, and came and ripped open my pockets to see what I had. This was her object from the first.

I had planned to start the next morning for Felton, but not before she had given me a good breakfast; and, after we came out of the lodging she gave me a glass, and, as we took it, she said, "You would think that I was a 'rum' creature last night." She asked me my name, and said, "If I would keep her and the child, she would make a good wife to me." I agreed that I would keep her a month, and, if we should cast out, that I never would be bad to the child.

We started for Felton, and she went on before me; when about four miles from Felton I called at a house, but they would give me nothing, and said that a blackguard of a lame beggar had almost killed his wife. I said, "I could not help that," and inquired "what they were like?" and I understood it was my new spouse, but I had no guess who the man was. I went on to Felton and got lodgings in the house of a tailor, and there was my last night's wife. If she claimed a man the night before, a man had now claimed her in earnest. He was lame and I was lame, but he was an old done man, and I am sure I could have thumped him. They had cast out, and she had determined not to remain long a widow.

I heard that a gentleman in Felton had come of age on that Saturday, and was giving a ball to the gentry, and holding great festivities. On the Sabbath morning when I rose, all the vagrants were up cooking their breakfast, to be off to the Hall. I determined to forestall them, and went to the door, and asked a woman how I would hold to the gentleman's hall. She directed me a short cut over a stile at the end of the town, which was a mile shorter than the turnpike road. I held on it, and soon had the gentleman's house in my eye.

A gentleman and two ladies made their appearance, and I thought I would try my hand upon them. It was the young gentleman and his two sisters; they halted, and put a few questions to me. The gentleman gave me half-a-sovereign, and from the ladies I received three-and-sixpence. I then turned to come off, but they told me to go on to the Hall, and see if there were anything there for me. I went, and was loaded like a "cuddy," and came back.

The rest of the cadgers, after breakfast, set out by the turnpike road, and it was fortunate for me that they took that road, for if they had taken the footpath they would have met me, and I would have been sure of a licking. I sold three shillings worth to the landlady. When the other cadgers arrived at the hall they were too late; and all they got among a dozen of them was not worth sixpence. When they returned they cursed their bad fortune for going, and considered me a wise man for stopping at home. I was glad they did not suspect my roguery.

I next day started for Alnwick, and there took lodgings in a barber's, whose wife is known among travellers, and goes by the name of "The Queen of ——." This woman is naturally belligerent, and peace is not agreeable to her disposition. When I went in I was warm, and asked "for a mouthful of water." She told me "that I might have it if I had a tin, and that I might buy one for twopence," as she said "she was not obliged to keep beggars in vessels."

I told her I rather considered "that the beggars kept her in vessels." Word followed word till a battle ensued, but the "Queen" gained the victory, as she broke my stilt over my head. She was not content with this, but went and called the constable, and I got a night in the black hole.

CHAPTER VI.

ON THE WAR PATH—BUFFY.

I WENT to Dunbar, where I remained a few days, and took the country by North Berwick; this is a fine little town, and the country round it is rich. I went along the coast to Prestonpans, and landed at Musselburgh, where I got 13s.; from this place I went on to Leith, sent to Edinburgh for books, and crossed to Kirkcaldy. This is a good town for a book, but very unchancy; in it there is an officer called "Waterloo;" he is an old soldier and an officious rascal.

I took lodgings at Pathhead, went to Kirkcaldy, and began to hold forth; "Waterloo" came up, ordered me out of the town, and said "that if he found me again about the place he would put me in the black hole." I said "if that was the case, he had better take me where I stood." With that he took me prisoner, and marched me to the black hole, where I lay all night.

Next morning I was brought before the magistrate, who was very severe, and asked me "where I belonged to? If I knew where I was born?" I said "I did." He told me "that was my parish." I said "Kirkcaldy is my parish, for my father and mother say I was born here." The magistrate asked my father's name, which I told him, adding "that they were Burghers, and that I was baptised by a Master Shirra in Kirkcaldy, and my tongue agreed with their tongue."

A gentleman, sitting near the magistrate, whispered something to him, when the magistrate wrote a line and handed it to "Waterloo," and ordered me to go with him. We went out together, and I got 5s., but, before we went, the magistrate told "Waterloo" that there was no need to be strict with a lame old man calling a paper on the street, provided there was nothing corrupt in it. "Waterloo" told me I might cry the town, which I did, and sold a great quantity of papers. It took me two days to cadge Kirkcaldy and the Links. I then went to Markinch, and stayed a week. There are three lodging-houses in Markinch; one was kept by a widow woman who could, on occasion, accommodate thirteen in her house.

Fifeshire, above all the shires in Scotland, is the place where a traveller will get a good bed; the reason of that is, that all those who keep lodgings are either old couples, who let beds to support them in the decline of life; or widow women, compelled to take that disagreeable step to help to bring up their families. A stranger in Fife has trouble in getting lodgings; as, to give Fife its due, its morals are less corrupted by the intrusion of strangers than any other county in Scotland, for they keep at a distance from strangers till they know them.

Travellers, for years back, pestered that shire, carrying a box and a bell in their hand, seeking bell-hanging or repairing umbrellas—although most of them knew as little about bell-hanging as I did; and, when they could not get a job, they were not sweared (slow) to commit burglaries. Cadgers have imposed more on this shire than on any other in Scotland.

One reason of that is because it lies convenient to Edinburgh, the seat of imposition; and, if hunted out of Edinburgh, they come to Fife, where they have a county with towns in it, the inhabitants of which are possessed with the noble principles of simplicity and charitableness; who never studied low deceit; and who would think it impossible for a mother to disable her child, with the view of assisting her in her begging excursions; or to send children out to steal, and beg, and then reset the stolen goods. You might expect nothing, but that the honest Fifers would say "that is surely beastly."

I went to Kennoway where I got a good quantity of meal, and sold it to a shoemaker by the slump; this man keeps pigs. Here I came to the door of a clergyman, who happened to answer the door himself. He asked me where I belonged to? That question I seldom answer in honesty, but that time it slipped out.

When I named the place, he stared, and asked me " What place there?" I gave him a look, and, doubting that he came from the same place, said, "that I was only a child when I left it, and could give no account of the place." He asked me to come in, but I would rather have been off. I I went in, and from my pretended ignorance of the place, although we were both at the one school, he never suspected me.

I did not return to Markinch that night, but snoozed in a outhouse, and next morning went to Leven. Lodgings are hard to find here, but I got into the house of a shear-grinder, who, with a woman from Perth had taken a house there, and had gathered together a few "scouring clouts," with which travellers, for their own accommodation, had to make themselves content. This is the worst place I met with in Fife.

Leven is a good small town, and from it I went and called Buckhaven. This town presents to the traveller from its situation, a picture of Scotland in ancient times; the houses are founded upon a rock, within the sea lash, and one cannot go from the one end of the town to the other without walking over rocks. There is neither cartway, nor footpath in the whole town.

From what I had heard of Buckhaven, I thought I would like to converse with its inhabitants, and, with this intention I entered a baker's shop. He knew me, as he had wrought in Edinburgh, and invited me in to rest myself. I went in and found a number of young fishermen in the house, with whom I began to converse, and found myself agreeably disappointed. They conversed on the history of Scotland, both civil and religious, with intelligence and power, so as to show that they were above the rank of the vulgar and thoughtless; and, on the subject of religion, they showed that they were not the dupes of clergymen and catechists, but the descendants of the ancient Bereans.

These fishermen had another *accomplishment* with which I was much delighted, as, when I was coming away, they all put their hands into their *pockets*. I called the village and found it charitable. I went to a large public work about half-a-mile from Buckhaven; it was at the dinner hour, and a number of youths were on the road meeting their friends. I was proud to see these youths, as I came forward, willing to share with me the morsel which they had for their dinner, and which was barely sufficient for themselves.

I refused the first, because I was not hungry, and considered that they required it as much as I did. A girl, apparently about ten or eleven years old, turned to her companions, saying, "Puir body, we'll gang and gar him tak' it, he'll no hae gotten nae denner yet." With that I was surrounded by about a dozen young girls, and had to take a share from all of them.

They all went on to the factory, and I came on behind. I went to the master's house, but here the scene changed. A girl came to the door, and, on seeing me, shook her head, saying with feeling, "Poor man, I have it not, and if I had I durst not give it to you." I might then have said with Home in "Douglas," "O Charity, where art thou to be found? surely thou dwellest not with the rich."

When I returned to Leven, I lodged in the same house with a beggar man, who was drawn through the country in a chariot by dogs; on the back of the chariot was a fox painted. This man sent to a merchant for thirteen sovereigns, for which he gave copper and silver, telling the merchant to whom he had given the change, "that he had been only out nine weeks, and had maintained himself, his dogs, and his boy, and cleared thirteen sovereigns." The merchant did not keep it a secret, and the news reached the authorities; in two days a "ban" was put on begging in Leven. I returned to Markinch, and then went to Leslie, where there was no lodging-house. I crossed the moor and came to Falkland, to the east of which lies Kettle.

Falkland is a royal burgh, and contains one of the ancient palaces of the Kings of Scotland; it is now in ruins, but from its appearance, it must have been one of the largest. It was burnt, but whether by Cromwell or the Covenanters, I forget. When I was going through the town I had a desire to see the palace, and I went and got myself drunk, as, when I am drunk, I have plenty of cheek, and will take no denial.

A gentleman, who is proprietor, has repaired the front square of the palace, but the other three squares stand in the most dejected ruin. In the square that has been rebuilt, stand statues of the family of the Stewart Kings of Scotland,

D

from James the First to James the Sixth; they are set in a stand along the front of the building. They are all entire, head and shoulders, with the exception of Mary the Queen, who is standing without the head.

I could not understand the meaning of this, as all the statues are made of the same stone. I enquired at an old man, how it happened that the Queen was headless? and he answered me, in a manner that I could not believe, "that a drop from the roof, lighting on her head, had by degrees worn it away till it was in its present state;" a most unlikely story. I fear that some rigid Covenanter has been the "*drop.*"

From Falkland I went to Auchtermuchty, and from thence to Auchterarder; as I went along the road I got my eye on a gentleman's house with a flag flying on the roof, and I thought I would see how things were rated there. I went to the kitchen, when a respectable-looking young woman appeared, and told me that "I had come on the wrong day; that the wedding was to-morrow." I understood that one of the gentleman's daughters was getting a husband. The servant brought me a large roasted bone, I doubt not but that it was 8 or 9 lbs. weight, and clumsy, but well picked.

I had a large bag in my pocket in which I placed the bone, got it on my back, and went off for Auchtermuchty. As I entered the town I looked out for the first public-house, which I entered, and "greased the wheels of life;" meeting with another, I determined to give the wheels another "coat;" by that time I was in marching order.

Having some books in my pocket, and finding the drouth continue at my heart, I determined on the speediest way to raise the wind. I pulled the books from my pocket and began to hold forth. I was soon surrounded by dozens, who gazed at me with both mouth and eyes; I was selling in good style, and finding myself very dry, I asked my congregation to preserve order for a few minutes, and I would return. I went and put a gill "in my neck," and returning, found my audience waiting patiently and anxiously for my return.

I addressed myself a second time to the Auchtermuchtonians, but had not got far, when the ban-beggar (town officer) entered the congregation, and intruded on our good order. He came crashing through the crowd, not without some love squeezes;

at last he presented himself before me, and, with the style and importance of his profession, addressed me in this manner,—"Sir, who authorised you to come here?"

I then made a stand, and, looking at him independently, told him "I had a roving commission, and considered it an insult on my authorities to be challenged by such an inferior as he was."

He then asked a sight of my authority, when I showed him my hand-staff, which, with a brass ferule on the end of it, weighed upwards of two pounds. I could see that my answer gave much satisfaction to my audience. " Buffy " determined not to be insulted, and told me that he would soon land me and my authorities in the black hole.

I said, " If he tried that, he would surely suffer for it."

He, being a stout-bodied man, would not stand the challenge, while the crowd was crying from every quarter, " You will be matched now, Flukemouth," for that was his nickname.

I, being three parts drunk, gave him a deal of insult, asking him " If he considered that the intention of employing such an abominable-looking man as he was for officer, was for the purpose of hunting beggars?" with such like chat.

" Buffy " got into a rage, he seized me, and I flung the stilts from me and got into grips with him. I could not stand and defend myself on one leg, but threw myself down, intending to get him with me on the ground, and give him a "proper pinning." He easily tumbled me to the ground, as it was my intention to be there; but being half-drunk, and getting angry, I forgot I had the bone on my back.

" Buffy " gave me a cast, and falling on my back, one of the spurs of the bone gave me such a stave that nearly took the heart from me, and for the moment I doubted the victory. I soon recovered, and seized him by the leg, while he was in the act of putting his hand in his pocket to bring out the handcuffs; I tumbled him, and he fell right above me; this gave me another sore wound in the back, from the bone.

A young man in the crowd, observing that the bone on my back was my strongest opponent, cried out, " give the lame man fair play." He cut the cord and took the bag off my back. Had it not been for this I certainly would have been in the " habble." I now gained freedom, and my care was always to be undermost, as, when I made a start pretending to get up, I got an opportunity of a blow or two at his face, on which occasion he shut his eyes. I gave him a pair of " decorated " eyes, and the cowardly rascal began to bite.

By this time it was not a running but a *rolling* fight. There was a burn on the one side, and a row of houses on the other ; with a fall from the street to the burn of from five to six feet perpendicular, and no dyke at the edge of the burn. We rolled about on the ground I sometimes exchanging a blow for his scratch, and he making a " haunch " with his teeth, till we came to the edge of the burn, over which I determined to tumble " happy-go-lucky."

When he saw himself on the brink, he attempted to extricate himself from my grip ; he rose to his knee, but I made another stroke at his face ; he jawed (tossed aside) his head to shun the blow, when I gave myself a " hist," and over we went into the burn, he pulling me along with him ; he lighted at the bottom, but I was cast furthest in.

There were large stones at the side to keep the water from encroaching on the street, on which he fell, and lay gasping. He had given me no quarter while I had the bone on my back, and I was determined that he should get as little from me. It was in the month of November, and the burn was swollen to the depth of from two to three feet.

While he was thrawing his face, and saying " he was gone," I was lying in the water on my elbow ; and replied, " You cannot be gone ; stand to the battle, at the worst it is only the death of a lame beggar, or of yourself ' Buffy ; ' and the beggar is a small loss to society."

With that I made a drive at him, when he fell from the stone on which he had rested, and I dragged him alongside of me. At this, bursts of laughter proceeded from the crowd, which by this time had become great, crying—" Well done old tar (for they took me for a sailor), give ' Flukey ' a dook (bath)." When, after a hard struggle, I with difficulty managed to get his head under water, and he was declared vanquished.

The crowd then gave me credit for my behaviour, and some men came in and lifted me out of the burn. As soon as I was brought on to the street " cordial " balsams were applied to me, which soon made me forget my wet skin. The crowd carried me to my lodgings, kept by a blind man, of the name of Stark, a relation of the townkeeper's; the people came in crowds, some giving me money, and others whisky, till I was *mortal drunk.*

The townkeeper had gone home and shifted himself, and, with an assistant, came to take me before the magistrate. I would have been made a prisoner, but the word spread through the neighbourhood, when the house was surrounded, and the "Buff" threatened on his peril not to "take me out of my lodgings that night as my clothes were wringing wet." He agreed to let me stay there that night, and bring me before the magistrate next day, who, he expected, would send me to Cupar.

Next morning by eight o'clock he was in my lodgings, lest I might make my escape. There were lodgers in the house who would have fallen foul of him, but I insisted on giving no more offence, and the lodging-house keeper started on him like a terrier, "Buffy" being a relation of her husband's; telling him, "That she was ashamed to put her head out of the door on account of him." The neighbours were gathering in the house, and "Buffy" would not let me wait for breakfast, but hurried me away, giving me a glass on the road, and took me to the magistrate.

I was doubting the worst, and assuring myself of getting confinement, for I knew I had done wrong by not going when ordered. The magistrate was a shopkeeper, and, when we arrived at his shop, a gentleman was with him, whom I took to be a writer, and they were conversing together. When we entered, the magistrate and the gentleman burst into a fit of laughter, and asked "Buffy" if his prisoner was self-delivered?

He told him that he "had apprehended me in my bed." They asked him "If I came peaceably?" He answered, "Yes." The gentlemen then told "Buffy" that he "might be very thankful that he did not get another dook" (bath).

The magistrate asked him, "How it took place?" When he told a long story, saying that, "I was calling blasphemy in the street; and that, when in discharge of his duty, he went forward to apprehend me, I had knocked him down with my stick," at the same time lifting the staff and showing it.

The gentleman who was with the magistrate interrupted him, saying, "He was there at the time, and saw him go forward and speak to me, when I lifted my staff and said, 'There is my authority,' and again laid it to the ground. More words were exchanged, when he saw 'Buff' seize me and throw me down, and all this time I had never attempted to resist." "Buff" declared, "That the gentleman had not spoken the truth."

By this time a crowd had gathered round the door, anxious to hear the result. The gentleman went to the door and asked, "If there was any person present who had seen the fight yesterday?" A number said, "They did;" and two respectable tradesmen were brought in who corroborated the gentleman's evidence.

The gentleman then told "Buff" that he would write to the Sheriff of Cupar, informing him of "Buff's conduct;" and stating "That instead of keeping the peace in that district, he was the only disorderly character in it."

When "Buffy" saw that all were against him, he only wished to have the matter settled, and asked to have authority to see me out of the district, naming another person to go with him and see me through Strathmiglo.

At this the magistrate looked at him, and, with a smile, said, "You think you would be afraid to go with him yourself; I am sure that the Sheriff will not pay an assistant."

"Buffy" then said he "would give a shilling himself." I said that "I would go peaceably with him if he would give me the shilling," which was agreed to before the magistrate, and we started. When he got me to the end of the town he gave me *fourpence*, and left me to my meditations.

I got into Strathmiglo, made a good thing, stayed all night, and next morning started for the "Nibs of Forth." This is a poor place; I could make nothing of it, and went on to Kinross, then to Lochgelly, and on to Crossgates. These places are all poor and hungry; Lochgelly is inhabited by colliers, who are poor, but charitable, and there is no money to be had from them except on pay-day.

CHAPTER VII.

IN FULL SWING.

IN Crossgates there is always a party or two of the real cairds, who keep the village in *fun* and the constables in *play*. One party—Grahams—could boast of their forefathers' existence in Fife for hundreds of years. The other party was Irish, of the name of Reilly.

An Irish fiddler named Brownlie, from Edinburgh, was in Crossgates, and, after breakfast, was going out to play the town. He took the badge of the Scottish "Blue Gown"* from his pocket and fixed it on his breast, saying, "I have this for my protection, and no thanks to the beggars in Scotland."

One of the Grahams, who was sitting on the floor mending a pot, said, "How did you come by that?" Brownlie replied, "It is here now, and no thanks to you." Graham said, "Certainly, a Scotch caird has a better right to it than an Irish fiddler."

Words created words, Graham took a hammer and broke the pot in twenty pieces, saying he "would do the same to any Irishman who would dare to wear the badge of Scotland."

So saying, he went and took a dram. Brownlie attempted to leave the town in haste, but the Grahams were not to be done; Graham whistled on his fingers, when all the Grahams of the caird order who were in the village turned out, cry-

---

* Paupers to whom the kings of Scotland were in the custom of distributing a certain alms; their number is equal to the number of years His Majesty had lived. Each "Bedesman" received a new cloak or gown of coarse cloth, the colour light blue, with a pewter badge, which conferred on him the general privilege of asking alms through all Scotland, all laws against beggary being suspended in favour of this privileged class. (*See Introduction to "The Antiquary.*")

ing, " Let the Irish blackguard who would dare to wear the badge of Scotland turn out."

By this time Brownlie was out of the town, and far on the Kinross road. Graham was not to be beaten; with as much fortitude and courage as the Knight of the Budget pursued the retreating son of Apollo, or as the Scottish Hero chased Edward from the field of Bannockburn, did our heroic caird pursue Brownlie, the " gut scraper " (fiddler).

When he came up with him, he " bade him several times of day " with the cudgel, while the " gut-scraper," on his knees, and with more earnestness than ever he was in at a Confessional, supplicated for mercy; but the caird, with the spirit which characterises his profession, determined to show no mercy, nor give quarter, till the son of the Green Isle would return what, he considered, Paddy had got by imposition from one of his countrymen. The fiddle was broken in pieces, and Graham bore the badge of the Thistle back in triumph to Crossgates, and went through the village with the medal on his breast.

But the badge was again contended for; the Reillys who had been in the neighbouring villages, and others in Dunfermline, assembled at Crossgates, and when night came on, with the assistance of a corps of tinkers, they determined to revenge the insult given to their fellow-countryman. The Grahams had a superior force, consisting of five stout men, and some *women*, who were most dangerous.

The Reillys' and Keiths' men approached the lodgings when we were in bed, and, with a smash, laid the door on its back. The encounter was general; the floor was covered instantly with men and women in battle-array; there was no alarm given, neither by bugle nor drum, and the garrison was taken by surprise, but the assailants found that they had the blood of the Grahams to deal with. The first salute was given to an old man at the fire; the weapon was iron; its use I know not, but its *effect* was convincing. Crowds of the natives, hearing the commotion, gathered at the door, and the battle was fierce.

A large pot full of porridge for the Grahams' supper was on the fire, and a young woman was in the act of making them. She seized a ladle, and, without grudging, divided them among the enemy; her well directed shot, if not lighting in the mouth, generally found the face. At the commencement of the encounter I was in bed, and was preparing to get up, but there was no way of getting *out*. I lay in the back of the bed, and, when the porridge was being divided, I covered myself with the blankets.

This was as coarse a scene as ever I witnessed; by chance there was no murder done, no blame to the well-aimed shots. There was not one of either party who could not show many wounds, besides being dreadfully scalded with the porridge. The Reillys and Keiths left Crossgates during the night, being afraid of the Grahams' connection.

Next morning Graham suspended the badge of the "Blue Gown" from his breast, and was determined to wear it. I told him, "if he wore it he would be taken for an Irishman, as Daniel Brownlie's name was on it." On hearing this he tore it from his neck, and was going to throw it into the fire, when we advised him rather to send it to Brownlie, seeing that it was of no use to any but him. After some hesitation Graham consented to return it, which was done.

I then went to Dunfermline; this is a good and charitable town. The town-keepers are very strict; the main street stands so high, that one can stand in the centre of it, and have all the principal shops in sight. I got the black hole from Saturday night till Monday; I had been travelling all day, and was feeling tired: a gentleman passed me, and gave me a shilling; after going on a little he turned and gave me two and sixpence. When I reached the end of Dunfermline I thought I could do no less than drink the giver's "health." I went into a public-house and did so, but, finding the drouth continue, I went into another and repeated the dose.

When I got to the lodgings I unharnessed myself, and went to a bookseller's named Miller, for ballads or histories, but he had nothing but tracts. These were a *bad fit*, but the drink being in the "garret" I took four dozen of them, went into the street, and began a long story. I soon gathered an audience, who relished the story, and many bought.

One of the buyers spurned his bargain, and challenged me for an impostor, saying I had given him "John Covey" in place of what I was calling. He demanded his halfpenny back, which I declined to do, and the crowd advised me to keep it. He went and told the town-keeper, who came and took me to the black hole. As soon as the town-keeper was off, whisky was handed in through the stanchions. I was drunk all the time I was in "quod," and, on Monday morning, the town-keeper released me, and ordered me out of the town.

I next went to Toryburn, and called two long villages; on the way between these villages I was passed by two young ladies, and, a little further on, I found a breastpin of gold, with a large and beautiful stone in it. I was sure it belonged to one of the young ladies, as it lay on the footpath where they had just been. I went on to Toryburn, and, having a drouth, went into a public-house, and got a gill.

I showed the landlady the pin, saying "I had found it on the footpath, and that as two young ladies had passed on before, I considered it belonged to them." She said "the two young ladies were her sisters, and she would give me a gill for finding it;" but I was too old to be caught in that trap. Before I left the house, she gave me 3s., and another gill.

I next went to Culross, which, like most of the ancient burghs of Scotland, is a hungry hole; and next day to Kincardine, and then to Alloa, where I stayed a few days. I found I was too near my own shores, and turned, and went by the foot of the Ochils, through the Yetts of Muckart by Glendevon, and arrived at Auchterarder. I had been in this place before, and was sure of lodgings; it was half-past nine at night, and I went to the door of an unmarried woman, who put up a young man, a namesake of my own, but the villain would not let her open the door.

Here was I, at a late hour, in a country town, ringing wet, and shivering of cold. A young woman came up and asked "if I wanted lodgings?" I said, "I did." She told me to follow her, and she went to the toll at the end of the town. I got lodging here, superior to the usual run of houses, but the woman who kept it had long served in gentlemens' families, and, her health failing, she was compelled to let it.

What was desirable to me, but not customary in that quarter, was a good fire, and I sent her out for a gill to revive my drooping spirits. After supper I went to bed, and she had my clothes dry in the morning; for which kindness I considered her entitled to a dram, and her breakfast.

This was Saturday, and I meant to stay in Auchterarder

till **Monday.** I went out and cadged the town, which is about a mile in length, and gathered twelve tankards of meal and eightpence halfpenny, besides a quantity of bread, with which I returned to the lodging. Four tankards I gave for my snooze, two I gave to bake, and four I sold. I gave the landlady sixpence to purchase barley, sugar, and tea with. With the rest of the money I went out to purchase beef, but lighted in a public-house, and "consumed" all but one penny.

I remembered I had to buy beef, and, resolving on my grand shift, I went through the town looking for a stationer's, but found none. I was returning, when I saw three men seated on a stone. One of them hailed me, saying, "When were you in Edinburgh?" "Ah!" thinks I, "I'm no' far afield yet;" so I went to them, and after some compliments, was presented with a large plateful of kail (broth), abounding with vegetables and Falkirk raisins (peas); with a good rams-horn spoon, I soon reduced its depth.

After that, they gave me a "glass," and asked me if I was "not going to give the folks of Auchterarder a story?" I said "I had no books, and could get none in the town." One of them said he "had seen me tell a good tale on an old newspaper." I said "I had none of them either." They soon found plenty, and, collecting a band of young men, I started.

The sale was good, and I did not fail in "greasing the wheels of life," till at last I was unable to stand, although able to speak. I was held up for some time, till a number of them brought a wheelbarrow, and seated me in it; I addressed the people from the barrow till I was past speaking, when they wheeled me to the toll where I was lodged. On seeing the crowd they shut the door, and refused to let me in, but the men from Edinburgh insisted on my admittance; the door was opened, I was carried upstairs, and the money counted, which amounted to 3s. On Sunday, when I understood my Saturday night's conduct, I was black with shame, and determined to leave the town.

On Monday morning I started by "grey" day for Muthill, which is a small village, the inhabitants of which are chiefly Highland people. They are very kind, and I did well there. That night I stayed at a country lodging-house, and next morning went to Crieff and called the town, which I found very hard. At night I took lodgings in a house in the street leading from Muthill. The house belonged to the woman that kept it, and consisted of two storeys. I asked the price of the lodging, and the landlady told me "tippence." I applied to the meal bag, when she turned out a tankard in which I could put my hand up to the elbow, till I heaped three tankards, which, I am conscious, contained three full pounds.

They had three rooms, and, at the rate of two in a bed, was ten tankards for every bed and shakedown; in each room there are four beds, which amounted to five pecks of meal at eight pounds per peck. I stayed here from Wednesday till the Monday following, taking Comrie and the country round. An old woman from Glasgow, was harnessing herself on the Saturday morning to go out; as she was leaving, the master and the mistress were seated at breakfast. The master, with a sneer, said : "Margaret, are you going to take no breakfast before you go out?" She said "she would not mind till she came in." Well did they know she had nothing to take, but they offered her nothing.

She returned in the afternoon, when she measured her meal and scrimply paid her lodgings. She had some pieces of bread and a small piece of salt beef, and, with a little coffee, she scrambled up a breakfast. As soon as the first cup was filled, she lifted it and the largest piece of bread and the piece of beef, and went to the landlady, saying, "Take that to ease your mouth." I had my own thought at the time.

That night I went to a bookseller's shop, and got four quires of the ballad of "Watty and Meg; or, The Wife Reformed," and started. The natives soon came round me, and, when I had a large congregation, I raised the price of the books to one penny a copy, and sold about a quire and a half. I purchased provisions, and came home about eleven at night. When I went in, the landlord challenged me for being late, but he soon found whom he had to deal with.

On producing the piece of meat I had bought, he changed his tune, and said, "You and us will make our kail together to-morrow." I told him that "travellers could not afford to mess with landlords, and they might make their broth as they pleased, and I would do the same."

Next day they would give me no coals to make my broth, although I was paying at the rate of sevenpence halfpenny a night; that was at the rate of fifteenpence a night for two, and sometimes they put three in a bed. As I would not make my broth with the landlady, although the beef and barley cost me fourpence, and only wanted a few vegetables, which they could have got from their garden; for spite they would give me no coals, expecting that, finding nothing to make it ready, I would give them a "thief's bargain" of it next day. But in that they were mistaken, for I went to a grocer's who found me in coals, and a travelling woman made the broth.

While we were at dinner she asked permission to give the woman, Margaret, from Glasgow, who had been so liberal to the landlady the night before, some of the broth, which I consented to do. With a few exceptions lodging-house keepers are robbing plunderers, and would skin the unfortunate wanderer without remorse; a thief is the most respected character at their fireside.

There was lodged here over Sunday three "dry-land" sailors and their fancy wives. I was leaving on the Monday, and it was fortunate for me, as there is no doing with these privateers while their purse-money is good.

CHAPTER VIII.

KITTLE COMPANY.

I STARTED on Monday morning for Perth, and that night I lodged in Methven, six miles from Perth. This is a fine little village, and I lifted ten tankards of meal in it, and some money. While calling the village I was informed, that the gentleman of Methven Castle had taken up a company of " mountain mariners." and sent them to Perth; I suspected they were our Crieff customers. I went that night to Perth, and took lodgings in one Dennis Bonar's, a fiddler, in the Meal Vennel. I did not know where I was, or who kept the lodgings, or I would not have called. The landlady was an old friend of mine, and, although a good-looking woman, was the most handless drab that ever I saw. I had her for three months. At that time Dennis was like to lose his wits about her, and I was glad of the opportunity of getting her off my hands; as one of her kind might have pleased a blind man, but would not suit me; so, in Paisley, I gave him my goodwill of her for a bottle of whisky.

They went from Paisley to the north, and settled in Perth, where Sally, like the most of Irish women that cannot work, started a lodging-house, and after that, a pawnbroker's shop and metal store, where she purchased everything that came in her way. These shifts were only for a time; she was accused of treating her husband in such a way that it terminated in his death; for this she was tried, but, the full charge not being proven, she got confinement, and is now wandering about the world houseless, and despised by all who knew her; but in her house, in the Meal Vennel, I lighted by accident, and got a kindly welcome.

I happened one day to get drunk, and began to cry the

town. I began at the end of the town that leads to Dunkeld, and had come only a small way inwards when I was seized and carried to the black hole; where I was kept from Friday till Monday, and put out of the town without being brought to a court.

In the hole where I was put, were two of our Crieff "mountain sailors." It appears that one of my companions named Gallacher, was passing for their captain, and that they were from St. John's in America, bound for Constantinople with fish; and were cast on the coast of Argyleshire, in Scotland. The captain and crew, carrying a pass from a magistrate in Campbeltown, were detected at Methven Castle, on Saturday.

The Fiscal's clerk, a boy about seventeen years of age, examined Captain Gallacher on his unfortunate voyage, he asked him "how long they were at sea when they were caught by the storm?" He replied "Five weeks." He was then asked "in what latitude and longitude he was, when the storm met him?" but to that question the Captain could give no answer. At last the clerk held out the pass to him, and offered to "let him out if he would read it," but that beat him. After the clerk went off, I began to chaff the Captain for not answering the questions, and declining to read the pass for his liberty.

A young man was brought in on Saturday night, intoxicated, and on Sabbath morning, when he was sober, the Captain asked his opinion of his case. I took the word out of the young man's mouth, and replied, "that the law of this country was *hanging* for all cases of forgery; and that for this crime, the King would give *no* reprieve; and, I added, that I was afraid it was a *cold morning* with him."

The lad corroborated this opinion, when the Captain, in the true Irish spirit, burst out with wild halloos, crying, "Ogh, Ogh, an' nee! and I'll be hanged, an' you think I will: and indade, and indade, I'll be hanged, and I'll never win out." I said "he would get out, but he would not be *long* out till he would be swung at the front of the jail."

On hearing this he again began the Irish halloo. The jailor, hearing the roars, opened the door, and asked the meaning of the disturbance. When, in wild distraction, the Irishman, wringing his hands, cried out, "they'll hang me, they'll hang me." The jailor asked him what he had done, and he replied, with a look, which denoted his terror, "I never did anything but beg."

The jailor said, "I thought you had been a seaman;" and the Captain said, "he had never been at sea in his life, and if he would let him out, he would never again pretend to be a seaman. The jailor telling him to hold his peace, and he would see what could be done for him to-morrow," went out and locked the door.

The Perth man told him that "what the jailor meant by that, was, that he would be brought before the Sheriff to-morrow, and then put in the iron room till he was tried; and then taken back and rivetted to the ground till he was hanged."

The Captain was now in more grief than when he was wrecked on the coast of Argyleshire, and again roared out bitterly. On hearing this, the jailor came and put him in solitary confinement, and the Perth man and I were left to ourselves. I saw Captain Gallacher no more for two years, when we met at a Fair between Aberdeen and Stone-haven, where he was standing with a party of thimble pitchers.

I arrived in Alyth and found it a tolerably large village. Here I fell in with Janet Cochran, a well-known character among travellers. I was calling the town and happened to be in a shop cracking to the goodman of the house, when in lighted Janet Cochran, and, making a low courtsey, paid her addresses, saying, "God bless you, sir, would you take pity on a poor widow and a fatherless bairn?" The man looked at her, and asked at her, "when her man died?" Janet said, "she did not ken."

Then, said the man, "the man may be living yet." Janet answered, "if he be, it is the better for himself, but are you going to give me anything?" The man said "he did not think that she was needing alms; she was young, and had but one child, and it was a poor hen that could not scrape for one bird."

Janet looked at him and said, "but are you going to give me anything?" He said again "he did not think she was needing charity." Janet then used an expression too vulgar to bear repetition, while the boy on her back, who had been pretending to be sleeping all this time, lifted up his head, and said, " aye, mother and mine tae."

I could not help laughing, and the man laughed too. Janet stepped out at the door, as unconcerned as if she had given no insult, but had paid him a compliment, and at night she came to the lodging-house where I was.

I arrived at Aberdeen about ten o'clock in the morning, and, after calling a piece of the town, I went and asked for lodgings, and was directed to Justice Port ; on arriving there I was taken to " Sinclair's Close." This close contains the rummest characters Aberdeen can produce. Here I lodged with a Highland woman who had five beds, three of which were occupied by women of the town, and the whole night the house went like a " Mearns Fair." I was aware of the situation, and made secure my clothes, not without occasion.

There were other two men sleeping in the same bed ; one of them left his clothes on a chair, and after he had got a sleep, he started out, saying,—" I had better look after my pockets ; " but, by that time, he had no pockets to look after, all was off. He then called to the landlady and asked her " if she knew anything of them ? " but she told him she " had not his clothes in custody, and he had better look for them where he laid them." They were all off, not an article was left, not so much as a shirt. He got into a passion, and began to abuse all around him. I then drew to my clothes, and, after harnessing myself, I went to the kitchen, where were a number of women round the fire,—the whole of them were tipsy.

Not suspecting that I knew the " cant," they were speaking about stealing the clothes. I sat and spoke back, and discovered where they were sold. The next morning, another man and I went to the house, which was in the Gallowgate. When we went in, the clothes of our neighbour-bedfellow, were lying on the counter. As soon as my neighbour got his eye on them, he claimed the garments, asking the broker " how he came by them ? "

I went out for a constable, but the broker sent his wife after me, and brought me back. The clothes were delivered, but I did not lift them from the counter till I went for the man to see what money he had. I went back and told him that " the clothes were found." The landlady asked me

E

"where we found them?" I answered, "that was a question which was unnecessary for her to ask, as she knew where they were, from the time they were lost." She followed me to the door, and asked me "what was to be done about them?" I told her that the person was a broker, and, as I was coming out, I heard the broker ordering the wife to go for a man of the name of "Dawson." As soon as she heard the name she cried out, and passed me like an arrow from a bow.

When I went to the Gallowgate, the landlady was there, offering to pay whatever was extracted from the pockets of the clothes. We returned to the man, who, for want of clothes was in bed. The landlady asked, "what money was in his pockets at the time he went to bed?" He said, "he did not care for his pockets, but he must have his coat." On it being produced, he examined the buttons on the breast, which were covered with cloth, and, after looking at them for some time, he said, he "believed all was right," and examined nothing else.

He put the coat on, and asked the other man and me out with him. He took us to a public-house, and asked us "what we would drink?" We told him "we considered we were not entitled to choose, or make demands, but, if he wished to give us a dram, just to call for it, as we considered that we, on finding his clothes, had only done what we expected he would do for us." He then told us that "his all was in his coat, and that he would drink a button."

With that he drew a button off the breast of his coat, and took off the cloth, when a sovereign presented itself. He then ordered a breakfast to be made ready for us; and, after that, the fuddle commenced. We drank that day and night, and the next day, and then we fell asleep, but there were more buttons than one taken off the coat. The next morning we were in a deplorable state. He wished to renew the fuddle, but we would not do so; he pulled off another button, and gave it between us.

I then went to a lane opposite the barracks, and asked for lodgings, and got them at the sign of the "Ship," where I found myself fully worse than in Sinclair's Close. For this was a house of bad fame in earnest. I was glad when I found it to be rising time, when I started, and was thankful to get out. I had been through a good part of England and Scotland, and have seen and heard a great deal, but this night crowned the whole. I then took lodgings in the Gallowgate, in a skulker's lodging-house, and kept *ordinary* quiet.

I consider Aberdeen, although not abounding in charitable institutions, is the most charitable city in Scotland. In the meanest door you can enter, if they cannot relieve you, they will appear sorry for it, and treat you civilly. In Aberdeen, as in all large towns, impostors have settled to a considerable amount, and, by degrees, will turn the heart of the city against cadging.

After residing in the Gallowgate for five weeks, I, with a number more went to a fair in Old Meldrum, and stayed in an alehouse. I was never out of Aberdeenshire for four months, and during that time, I travelled the banks of the Dee and Don on each side of the city, upwards of thirty miles; it is a matchless county for charity, and is sorely imposed on.

In the course of my travels in Aberdeenshire, I fell in with a piper who was shamming madness. He was dressed in tartan, with a bonnet and feathers, the pipes had no chanter, and skirled only with the drone. He and I entered into a joint-stock connection, and the firm existed six weeks. I led him, pretending that he was deaf, dumb, and blind, and he gave the best proofs of being crazy; in this way we managed to extort, both fun and a good living.

As we drew near the door of a farm-house, he, in general, started the drone, and played forward, and, by the time we got the length of the door, the inmates were all astir; we were usually asked into the house, where we gave them both fun and roguery for their charity.

In the course of our travels, we came to the Earl of Aboyne's, and got in at the gate, unknown to the porter. After searching for the kitchen, we came up to the front door, I bad him play up " Johnny Cope," and with his drone, he did as well as he could. During the music, there were repeated raps on the window, signifying that we were to retire, but the more they rapped, the more I encouraged him to play up, and stick by " Johnny Cope," till at last, they put up the window and pitched over half-a-crown, ordering us "never to enter the gate again."   The Countess of Aboyne was the *daughter* of Sir John Cope, but the piper did not know this.

In a few days after that, we fell in with a woman on the cadge ; she was about the age of thirty.   This woman captivated the heart of the piper, and he asked my assistance in the courtship.   I gave him all the assistance possible, but all the while doubted her to be a rogue: however we stuck together for some days, and during that time we were spending hard, but I resolved to bring her to the scratch.   So we came to a public-house, and I gave him the hint that I would strike up the connection, if they would now settle it without going any farther.

We went in and commenced the fuddle, and, after spending almost a pound, the people in the public-house objected to giving them a bed ; so I insisted that they would give her a bed in the house, and he and I a bed in the barn, to which they agreed.   I told him that I was meaning to leave the connection the next morning, which I did, and, by myself, travelled fourteen or fifteen days in the district.

In the parish of " Braemar " I met my piper, who, the night I left them, had made up the marriage with the woman. After a union of three days, she made an elopment with all the money he possessed, and the pipes into the bargain, not even a meal bag was left.   When me met, the piper was almost in a state of despair ; we sat down, and in broken English he gave me a statement of his love adventures ; but when he came to the manner in which she left him, he fell through the English and *tore* at " the tartan," threshing on the earth with his staff, till I began to think he was really daft.

After he had given vent to his passion of grief, we began to take into consideration what tack we would next pursue. I proposed to him to act the madman, but he rather preferred the "' deaf and dumb line," which I was sure he was not able for, but he insisted, and I yielded ; so we agreed for him to play " dummy," and me to explain ; and we again went partners, but not without charging neither to speak or laugh in the time of transacting business, whatever might take place. So we went in search of a job.

The first house we came to, we went in, and, after he made

the signs, a tittering began among some of the young lads
and lassies.   One of them came with a bowl full of meal, and
pointed to the back of the house; we went off, and, when
turning the corner of the house, we saw, on the rise of a
knowe, a cot-house; it was occupied by the shepherd of the
farm; we went up to it, and were scarcely in, till we were
followed by two lads and lassies, who entered laughing, and
asked me if that man was dumb.

I told them "he had been dumb from his birth, and had
proved himself to be possessed of supernatural knowledge, in
the presence of both ministers and magistrates." So we
made a bargain, and he began to chalk on a chair, and I to
explain; and, from what I could borrow from their own
observations, I was appearing to gratify their wishes. Un-
fortunately, the herd came in, and, after looking a while,
touched the "dummy" on the shoulder, saying, "what have
you made of the pipes?" at which the dummy burst out
laughing, and said, "I do not know."

I was making for the door when one of the lads brought
me back; I was afraid of a "habble," and ordered "dummy"
to give back the shilling that he had received, but he swore
"he would sooner be shot." The lassies looked as if they
had been elf-shot, but asserted, that whether he was dumb
or not, I had told them what they knew to be true, and they
were sure that one of us kent something. So the whole of
them insisted that we would go on with the prophesying,
but I still doubted the end of it; however, we made good
2s. 3d., and came off with flying colours.

After we went out the herd followed us, and gave us a
hint about a young woman that was in love with a young
man, and gave us some hints of their conduct. With that
we went off and got the young woman by herself. The bargain was struck; the piper marking with his chalk, and me
improving on the information given by the herd; and in
both of the attempts we came off with success.

In this "line" we travelled a few weeks, but I could not
be bothered with him, and I determined to part with him
so. He proposed to try another "line," and we set out again,
he acting the half-crazy man. I held on to Aberdeen, and
in a few days reached it; here I continued two months, and
lodged in the "Bowl Row," and then I came south to Ber-

wick; from it I went to Belford (in Northumberland), a distance of fourteen or fifteen miles. It is a poor village, but a rich country round. Travellers can stay here for nights, and find country and villages for hawking without touching the road.

Although Belford at that time contained seventeen beds, besides makeshifts (each bed and makeshift containing a couple of persons, if not three, at threepence a head), that night I could not find a spot in a lodging-house, and was obliged to apply to the overseer, who was good enough to give me a line to their charity hospital, where I was received for that night. When I went in, it was about nine in the evening; in a little after, I was brought a plate of " crowdy." This is made by putting a quantity of raw, round meal into the vessel, pouring on boiling water, and stirring it round till it turned as thick as a pudding, and, mixed with butter or kitchen fee, it makes a strong feed. I got milk to my " crowdy," which did very well.

I was told by the governor that the inmates had supped on the same. This hospital was a self-contained house, and I guessed its inmates to be from thirty to forty—a few old and infirm, a number of lunatics, and the rest youths, chiefly girls, of a clean and healthy appearance, which certainly did credit to the governor, as I understood the hospital was " rouped " yearly to the lowest bidder.

CHAPTER IX.

THE " INS " AND " OUTS " OF BEGGING.

NEXT morning they gave me my breakfast of porridge and milk, and I proceeded down the coast by Bamborough Castle, taking the villages as I went. This was bad ground for lodgings, as there is not lodgings from Belford to Alnwick. I visited Bamborough Castle, which is situated on the sea-side; there are a number of inhabitants within it, and it contains shops of cloth, hardware, &c. Near to it I passed the night in a pigstye. Next day I called at two villages but got no lodgings.

A wife, with a deal of humanity put me into a house that had only part of the roof on, and gave me two sacks and some straw. Next day I got up to Lord Gray's Castle, where I got a great quantity of victuals, which I carried to the village and sold. I then proceeded to Alnwick—the last time I was there I was glad to get out of it,—and travelled to Newcastle, holding my way through the north border of England by Hexham, but, when I arrived there, on account of some misdemeanour committed by supposed travellers, they were taking up every person having the appearance of *travellers*.

I neither can nor will justify the conduct of travellers in cases of petty theft committed in houses, as often daughters and servant girls are the guilty persons; as in the case of fortune-telling, which in general is paid at the family's expense, and that at the dearest rate. Likewise " bowl-hawkers," who, when servant girls break any article by misfortune, they arrange with a " bowl-hawker," when it is replaced at the expense of some other article going amissing.

" Bowl-hawkers," in general, carry privately along with them tea and whisky, which they can dispose of to great advantage among weavers. They exchange these articles for yarn both in country and town. Often the wife of the labourer trafficks with the "bowl-hawker" for his or her contraband articles, and pays them from the meal barrel, with the hard earned industry of the husband. The servants deal with them at the expense of their honesty, and to the serious hurt of the families whom they serve.

When any petty theft is discovered, there are instantly suspicions lodged against some beggar or beggars, when a prosecution is started against that class of vagrants, whom I will not clear, as I am confident there are a great number of them thieves, who ask charity as a means of stealing; but I am aware that "bowl-hawkers" have, by ten degrees, a greater opportunity to be thieves and resetters.

I am well aware of the roguery of begging, and that a great number of them are mean impositions, by the exposure of pretended diseases, which are practised both by males and females in a disgraceful manner; and not only so, but these impostors bring up their children in the same manner. Still, the "bowl-hawker" is, of the two professions, the most dangerous; were he to purchase his articles, hawk and sell them, on the profit allowed, they could not keep themselves in tobacco. It is by their *barter* they live, which, indisputably, must be imposition.

There is another kind of vagrant impostors; I mean hawkers for old clothes. Their real title is "Rob the beggar." These impostors go to work two or three in company, one on each side of a street, a third stands in the street inquiring at the passengers for old articles. When a person presents an article before the old clothesman, he carefully overhauls it, and points out its defects to reduce its esteem with the exposer. Then he appears not to be disposed to have it: but by way of charity gives a bode that never comes within a third of its worth. If the bargain be struck, good and well; if not, he sends his partner, perhaps next day, inquiring for old articles; if the exposer presents his article, and tells what was offered, he laughs at them, declaring the bidder "a fool."

Yet these great impostors are never mentioned in the numbers that are turned over for prosecution, but all must light on the beggar. The blind, the lame, and the aged must be expelled the streets, driven into black holes, and shut up in Bridewells, while screaming impostors pass unnoticed, and laugh at the punishment of the lame, blind and aged.

I came to Ferrytown of Cree, which is a poor town, containing a few one-storeyed, thatched houses, occupied mostly by Irish families, the most of whom support idleness at the expense of misery. As I entered the village I was accosted by several men and children, asking if I wanted lodgings. That is a bad sign; I therefore declined the whole of the offers.

At last, a woman with a basket came up and offered a bed at 3d. a-night. I went with her and was agreeably disappointed in finding a good lodging, fire and bed. There is no use of a traveller calling this village, as one third of the inhabitants are all beggars. I therefore started for Newton-Stewart, about six or seven miles distant. This is a smart and good town, containing shops of all descriptions; it consists of one street, being a row of houses on each side of about three-quarters of a mile in length, with another street leading to the Ferrytown of Cree. It is good work for a cadger, and is worth, on an average, from 3s. 6d. to 4s.

In most places in Galloway the "farm" lodgings are against the common lodging-houses, as the travellers seldom come to these in this district except when selling, or on a cold or wet night. There are a great number of beggars, but all are of the lazy cast, and, when coming from their rounds, few lodging-houses will admit them, as it is impossible they can be clean, and, although I am a beggar, I would scarce feed a dog with the scraps of food that they carry, after cadging with it on their back through the day, with a child riding above it, and lying under their heads for a pillow at night. Yet, I often wondered to see in lodging-houses, respectable women demeaning themselves to purchase and offer to any person, the articles they would not use themselves. In Galloway, it would be hard to estimate either the number of beggars or the expense of their support.

I left Newton-Stewart and came to Glenluce; this is a small moorland village, poor, but charitable. It is famous as the burying-place of the celebrated "Michael Scott," whose memory will be ever dear to those who cherish the recital of witch and fairy tales.

I proceeded to Stranraer, which is the largest town in the county. I had "called" it before. I do not know how to term this place, as it contains an Ireland—a Dublin and a Belfast—of its own. The first time I visited it was on a Saturday. Their own poor, as they called them, were calling the town, who, by appearance were all Irish. The answer I got at almost every door was, " We serve none but our own poor." I thought I was never to get one halfpenny, but at last I got twopence, and went to a bookseller's shop, where I found a few quires of " Watty and Meg." I went and started the town, and in less than an hour I had upwards of five shillings.

By this time it was getting far on in the afternoon, so I recruited my stock, and held forth a " Cure for ill wives," knowing that if I did not sell that night, I would have little chance on Monday ; so I continued till on the border of 10 o'clock, when I had sold nigh to three quires, and by that means made up an ill day's cadge. I halted here for some days, and then, travelling by the Carron and Ballantrae road, I came to Girvan.

This is a large village, consisting of several streets There are none in this town, from the minister downwards, that do not earn their daily bread. There are near 2000 looms in the village, which is very poor. Three-fourths of the inhabitants are Irish. Considering their poverty, they are really charitable. A cadger will find far more charity in Girvan, in its present state, than if three-fourths of them were gentry. I think I can defy the three kingdoms to produce a town of the same kind in size and numbers, with neither gentry nor middle class. An ordinary beggar can cadge in Girvan from twelve to sixteen tankards of meal, and, in the season of the year, two or three pecks of potatoes. There are a number of lodging-houses in Girvan, but I cannot say to what amount.

I started from Girvan by Dailly and Garpel Bridge for Maybole. On this route there are some good gentlemen's houses, and on the way I picked up about 4s., and plenty of scraps. On arriving at Maybole, I took up my lodgings nigh to the old college, in the house of a weaver. I had long meditated how the trade of "bowl-wife" might be destroyed but in this house I saw it was of no use to bother myself any longer in that pursuit. I could find a way to extirpate every other low villany, but that beat me. I found that the trade could be carried on independent of "bowl-hawkers." This is a town of considerable size, and the capital of that district of Ayrshire called "Carrick." There are a number of tolerably wealthy families in Maybole, but in charity it can never be compared with Girvan.

From Maybole I proceeded to Ayr. This town consists of the "Old" and "New" towns. The old town of Ayr contains a number of respectable families, and is very charitable. There are a number of most respectable shops of every kind in the old town, and some elegant gentlemen's lodgings. There is also a new jail, containing County Hall and Clerk's rooms, besides accommodation for debtors and felons; of which accommodation cadgers sometimes receive a share.

A few years back, at the expense of the town, they took down the old tower of "Sir William Wallace," and rebuilt it in an elegant style, with the figure of the Scottish Patriot cut out in stone upwards of seven feet high. His appearance is about thirty years of age, leaning on his sword, and his face turned toward the south, as if on the look-out for Southerners.

In this monument to the memory of the great and unselfinterested hero, the worthies of Ayrshire, have cleared themselves of ingratitude to the memory of that noble character, whose name ought, and shall be, held in everlasting remembrance, not by Scotsmen alone, but by men of every clime, in whose bosoms is instilled the love of country, Englishmen not excepted, who, although he was their enemy, respect his memory.

There are many towns in Scotland, abler by way of cash than Ayr, and in whose neighbourhood, he achieved deeds qualified to immortalise him, where, to the present generation, his memory is only called into existence by old wives, about their fireside, among the children of the neighbourhood, when his great exploits get their turn among the stories about witches, warlocks, fairies, and brownies. Stirling is one of the towns that has shown a barren spirit towards the deeds of that hero, as their shire can, in many places, show the fields where he and his warriors drew their swords, and with their blood, stained the heather for their enthralled countrymen. For instance, the battle of Stirling Haughs, and the drawbridge about a mile-and-a-half west of the Castle. *

The battle of Falkirk has nothing to keep alive its memory but a large stone on a rise in the moor, about three miles south of Falkirk, known by the inhabitants in the neighbourhood by the name of " Wallace's Stone." This stone is, I think, from 9 to 10 feet in height, and may be in weight 7 or 8 tons.

The inhabitants of that neighbourhood tell that, when the battle was going on, Wallace was at a loss to see the manœuvres of the two armies, and went to a small rivulet, about half-a-mile distant, lifted this stone and carried it in his "oxter" (under his arm), to the brow of the "brae," where he set it on its end, mounted it, and from its height oversaw the battle. This " Ebenezer" of Wallace, which to me is as absurd as " Alladin's Lamp," is all the proof that Stirlingshire can give of his achievements.

The new town of Ayr stands on a good space of ground, and a good many streets of it belong to the parish of " St. Quivox." Its inhabitants are mostly colliers. There are a number of lodging-houses in the old town, but the most of travellers resort to the new town. The reason for that is, *because the new town keeps no black hole.* There is always a great number of beggars. If there is a family of them, they can do well, and numbers of them pass the winter here ; the husband going out by himself, or perhaps working ; the wife going out with the small "kids," the oldest of them with "spunks." The old bridge is an excellent begging stance on the Friday and Saturday nights.

Between lurkers and travellers, young and old, they may be estimated on an average at fifty. The lodging here is in general twopence.

* The massive " Wallace Monument," on the Abbey Craig, near Stirling, has been erected since " Hawkie's " day. Should he not be ranked amongst the early *movers* in that matter ?

CHAPTER X.

"A CHIEL'S AMANG YOU TAKING NOTES."

LEAVING Ayr late in the afternoon, I stayed about three miles from it, at a place called Prestwick. This is but a small village, but is the most ancient borough in Ayrshire. Its authorities were once great, but the Council sold their rights, piece by piece. It is governed by a provost, three magistrates, town councillors, and thirty-six freemen, who, according to their charter, rank as *lords* within the royalty. A "freedom" there sells sometimes at £600; this "freehold" can be sold only to the Council, who, in general, purchase it for a mere trifle.

The liberties of a freeman are the possession of a given number of acres of arable land. Each freeman is entitled to keep, on a common belonging to the borough, two cows, a stirk, a calf, and a horse, three days each week; with an equal right to gather wrack on the shore, which is the best manure that can be put upon that ground, as it has a sea-sand foundation, which makes sea-weed pulverize.

This borough has an institution bequeathed by King Robert the Bruce. I never read of it in history, but, by strict inquiry at intelligent persons in the borough, whose accounts carry consistence, I was informed that the narrative runs thus:

King Robert, flying from the Southerners, and feeling much fatigued, laid himself down and fell asleep within the boundaries of this borough, among the hills of sand by the sea-side. After some time he awoke and found himself covered all over with leprosy, and faint with thirst, which increased to such a degree that he was unable to go in search of water. He resigned himself to death, and drawing his sword from his side, he stuck it in the sand, when, to his surprise, there issued forth a spring of water of which he drank, and then bathed himself in it, when the leprosy left him ; after which he prosecuted his journey.

When he was in possession of the kingdom, in thankfulness for his deliverance, he caused a chapel to be built on the spot, which was called King's Ease ; the ruins of it can yet be pointed out.   The well yet stands, and is called King's Ease.   He also founded an institution on the spot for lepers, to the number of fifteen.   Their endowment was a hut made of sand, with a piece of ground to each for a garden, with seven bolls of meal, and one shilling for every boll, to purchase salt.

The meal and shilling he left a burden on lands in the parish of " Dundonald," at a place called the " Loans."   The holder of the land had to deliver the meal and shillings at their place free of expense.   The Institution existed for near five hundred years, but, about forty years back, the unthinking freemen of Prestwick sold that noble institution to Ayr Charity Hospital, for the paltry sum of £20.

By the time that it was sold, admittance to the " Foundation" was refused, and only two persons were on the Institution, both residing in the village of Prestwick.   The name of the one was Robert Kerr, and of the other, Ann Miller. These were both living in the year 1825 ; their charter was a stone of a peculiar shape, which was laid within the chapel ground while it was in repair.   The well and stone were considered sacred, and were of much value to the clergy, but a low character of the name of Allison, who rented a salt-pan in the neighbourhood, about the year 1800 bribed a drunk man, who broke the stone in pieces.

Thus an institution perished that might have supported, in the borough of Prestwick, a great number of infirm persons in an hospital, that would have done an honour to the borough, and would, in many respects, have better preserved the memory of the great deliverer of Scotland.

I then found my way to Kilmarnock, for trade and size, the principal town in Ayrshire.   This is a good town for every kind of traveller, and numbers of cadgers make it their residence for three or four months at a stretch ; but their want and profligacy incurred the displeasure of the inhabitants, who, from time to time, made open displays against their irregularities.

Warnings by black hole and banishment from the borough had no effect on them, when at last a notorious character, a blind Irishman of the name of James Kenny (who, although blind, was one of the worst characters going), had fallen in with a woman in Irvine, who, although begging charity, could turn to any shift to make money, and agreed with this blind man to go with him to Kilmarnock for her supper, bed, breakfast, and a shilling. But she, being up to her trade, rumbled his pockets in the dark, and decamped with a sovereign. When he found that she had run off he declared himself robbed, and asked the police of the town to assist in apprehending her. When they apprehended her she was drinking in a tavern, and had only spent a trifle of the sovereign.

She was brought before a magistrate ; when the case was investigated, the magistrate considered that, when a beggar could afford to offer her what Kenny did, be robbed of such a sum, and afterwards apply to him for *justice* in the case, it was time to put a stop to beggars in the borough.

This act was a great loss to travellers of every description, as Kilmarnock was a good town for *them*. I may state that above fifty beggars, ballad singers, and speech criers, loitered daily about that town, till this circumstance took place ; and, since that time, not one of them has received a day's indulgence. A town "lurker" has all the chance, as they know the town, and make themselves acquainted to such a degree, that they pass unnoticed. A lurker *travelling*, particularly in winter, can take the shops unnoticed, and do well ; as this system is not practised by the meal-bag beggar, and the person cadging under the pretence of being a tradesman, must always go better clothed and cleaner, than a cadger bearing meal-bags, &c.

Before that case of the blind man's, which put an end to cadging here, either man or woman, who were only cadgers without lurking, could, any night, gather nine or ten tankards of meal, besides money and scraps.

This is a great town for shop-lifting, which is practised by a number of drunken women belonging to the place. They can execute their business on as crafty a scale as the most travelled rogue. While I lodged in the Foregate with Mrs Bicket, and in " Little Paddey's " in the same street, I found out the source of the bargains they were offering, particularly on the Saturdays; and yet, a number of them passed for decent women.

Here I fell in with a woman from Leith. We agreed to travel in company to Greenock, and we came to Irvine, where we stopped three nights. This is a good town for travellers, but when they commit depredations, the town is obliged to turn strict for some time. This place can stand travellers three days a week, together, with Fullerton, from which it is divided only by a bridge, and is generally " called " by travellers while they reside in Irvine; and, if they take the coal works in the neighbourhood, their residence in Irvine stands a week, and can afford them no idle time.

With my new partner I then travelled to Kilwinning, a distance of three miles. This town must be taken soon in the morning, or the cadger will come little speed, as the " salt-pan " cadgers can start and run six miles, and call a tolerable village before breakfast time. Kilwinning stands the cadger from ten to twelve tankards of meal, besides odds and ends.

Here some queer vagaries of my new wife threw the town into an uproar, and with sorrow I saw her " in the hands of the Philistines." I was thankful when I got through the crowd unsuspected.

I arrived in Greenock, and lodged in the Highland Close. They set four beds, and had a number of bowl-merchants living among them. There were a brother and two sisters from Connaught. Had they had a spirit above meanness, I might have bestowed the name of a man and two women on them; but, when I saw a stout young man about the age of twenty, combing and curling his hair, for the purpose of running the world with a rag-pock on his back, collecting all the abominable off-scouring that families consider unfit to keep about them; while in a dashing manner he walks from door to door, carrying in one hand a water-jug, and over the other arm a basket of bowls.

Thus equipped, he considers himself a merchant, and not of the ordinary sort. Among his own kind he is held as a respectable person, and he assures himself of the truth of it. His sisters decked in the old articles they had lifted as rags, appeared as proud of their calling as if it had been the most respectable in the country; and they could talk about lads with as much impudence as if they had been qualified for a wife, a mother, and a house-keeper.

Here I stayed for a fortnight, and during that time I cadged the town every day, and on the Saturday nights I sold books to enable me to keep the Sabbath day. During the time that I stayed in that house, these bowl-dealers sold better than £6 worth of old clothes to an Irish dealer, and they were in a fair way for making money; but, as every day, something went amissing with the lodgers, I left the house, and went to lodge near the mid-quay. This house kept five beds, and I stayed here nine weeks; during that time I sold two reams of books at a penny each copy. I cadged during that time only once at Greenock, and once at Helensburgh. This house was a great resort for travellers, and Greenock is a very generous town.

I then went from Greenock to Port-Glasgow, where I stayed a few days; this is a good town for its size, and I did well. A cadger can continue here two days and do well. I afterwards tried to sell some of my books at a penny each, as at Greenock. This town, Port-Glasgow, stands a cadger from three to four shillings in an ordinary way. There are three lodging-houses in it, besides two or three widow women, that let beds. But the " Port," in general, is "called" by travellers while residing in Greenock.

I sailed from Port-Glasgow to the Isle of Bute; there were other three vagrants in the same boat. We were scarcely ashore at Rothesay, when the town-keeper marched us all to the black hole, where he kept us till the boat returned, and sent us back. This adventure was not so pleasant as we would have wished. We were again landed at Greenock quay; I made *some noise* in the town, which called the people's attention, but I returned to the quay and went on board the first boat for Helensburgh, where I stayed all night. I only "called" the town with books, and next day started for Dumbarton.

This is a town that needs no townkeeper, at least for a cadger, as it appears that amongst the inhabitants there exists a strict union against cadgers. I "called" the town, and the Bridgend, and could scarcely treat myself to a glass of whisky when I had done my cadging. I then gave it up, and meant

F

to come to Glasgow; but next morning I went to Bonhill, and did well, both in cadging and crying. I took "country quarters" a little out of Bonhill; and next day crossed over to Renton, which I cadged, and cried; and next day returned to Dumbarton. From Dumbarton I went to Kilpatrick, calling at Milton and Bowling, and gathered some meal and "bawbees." I stayed three nights in Kilpatrick, and "called" Milngavie and Glenhead. In the two last villages, there was no lodgings, and I had to return each night to Kilpatrick.

At Renfrew I crossed the water, and went by Paisley. On the road I fell in with a "dry land" sailor who was going that way. He told me that there was a sailors' box in Renfrew, that relieved sailors belonging to the Clyde who were in distress, with from 2s. 6d. to 3s. 6d.; and if I would go along with him, he would give me a share of it. I was willing enough to be rogue, but neither he nor I being seamen, I would not venture. He went himself, and received 3s. 6d. When he returned, he laughed at me, and told me that he was examined by an old weaver who knew nothing about the sea, and gave him the money on sight of his pass.

I "called" Renfrew, but found it a very hard town. I did little more than clear my way, and proceeded to Paisley, where I lodged at the Sneddon Bridge. There are a number of lodging houses in this neighbourhood of the most ordinary sort. I lodged in different houses there, and in them were to be found boys and girls, calling themselves "drawboys," out of work. They all could speak "cant," and were in the habit of coming in *very late*. Paisley supports a great number of vagrants of every description. It is a seat where cairds of all different orders can be found, and menders of bellows, pots, or pans.

CHAPTER XI.

"ROGUES IN ALL TRADES."

FORTUNE-TELLERS are much encouraged among the females; while residing at the Sneddon Bridge there were two fortune-tellers in the same house, who, if they had been careful, and if money got in that way could prosper, might soon have built houses. But it was got in the most horrid manner, and only served the purpose of stupefying their judgment, and keeping the place where they resided in perpetual confusion.

There was a pair of blankets taken from a bed, which led to a scene of trouble; every individual in the house charged one another with the crime; the landlady obtained a Bible, and made all swear on it that they were honest; she also resorted to the desperate experiment of which is called " Turning the Key." (*See page* 26.)

The most of lodging-houses are kept by Roman Catholics, and if they are good and attend the church regularly, they are the most honest of all lodging-house keepers. If an article was left in their charge, you might call twelve months after, and get it as you left it; but those who did not attend their church, in general stood at nothing. This of itself proved the grandeur of religion, and the virtue of appearing before God at a confessional. I got the "kick" from my landlady in this lodging, on account of a young man who came from Johnstone, in the character of a daft man; he was the completest in that line I ever met with. He was three nights in the house before I knew what he was about; but I kept an eye on him through the town, and he could play his part well.

As I passed him in the Square, I convinced him that I was suspicious of him. To give him justice, he could act daftness with any I ever saw. That night, when supper was over, and the house was preparing for bed; the fellow kneeled down at a chair in pretence of praying. I was sitting at the fireside when I saw him on his knees; I lifted my staff, and gave him a rap over the rumple, saying "Get up you devil's servant! Do not dare in my presence to go sneaking through the country all day, begging and imposing on the public, pretending insanity, and to address God at night in prayer."

He started to his feet, and the landlady got into a rage, declaring that "it was not right of any Christian to keep me about the house, for insulting a person on their knees at prayer." I justified myself, but she refused all reason. I saw it was in vain to dispute, and next morning I left the house.

I then went and lodged in Sawpit Street with an Irishman of the name of "Colin Thom." He kept the largest lodging in Johnstone. From that I "called" the "Slates" and Elderslie, where I got seven tankards of meal. Next day I went to Kilbarchan; this is a village of considerable size, but it consists chiefly of weavers; at this time their trade was very flat, and I made very little. Next day I went to Crossley Mill, and Houston Village, and made upwards of twelve tankards of meal, but the pennies were scarce.

I went and stayed that night at the Bridge-of-Weir; the inhabitants of this village all work in cotton factories, but sometimes suffer much for want of water. I "called" part of the village and returned to Johnstone. This is now a village containing, I suppose, from seven to eight thousand inhabitants, and about sixty years back, it consisted only of one thatched house. This is the result of commerce.

At this time there was eight lodging-houses in Johnstone, and between beggars, "spunk" (the old form of "lucifer" matches) dealers, bowl-merchants, tinkers, and ballad singers, we may count forty vagrants living on the three parishes of Johnstone, Kilbarchan, and Houston. The expense of their support may be estimated at 2s. a day, making a sum of £4 among the three, not counting a lodging in Kilbarchan, another in Bridge-of-Weir, and likewise travellers from Paisley.

If this statement were taken from my cadging, the half of the amount would be sufficient; but I, being lame, had to content myself with the low doors, when *"up-stairs"* was the best chance. Neither was I able to go over the half of the ground that a stout man or woman with both legs could do.

A "spunk" merchant in that neighbourhood would consider himself broken if he could not bring home a peck and a half of meal, besides a burden of potatoes, often selling 2s. worth of "spunks." A ballad singer thinks nothing of drawing 2s. at the "scale" of the public works, and pays one penny for the dozen of the ballads. A bowl-dealer, in a weaver's house, can sometimes lift as much as 2s. worth at once, besides his plunder in old clothes and cotton waste, and this is within the bounds. I would wish a begging stance on the road on Saturday afternoons, between Paisley and Johnstone, as it is worth from 2s. 6d. to 3s. a day, and, if extreme objects, who can lay out their case in a pitiful way, it is worth far more.

The last time that I was on that road, a Connaught woman was sitting with four children, and a bed laid down for the young ones. Her tongue was going like a bell, bawling out "Help the Widow and Orphans" (who never had husband or child). At night she counted 14s., besides having had drink; only paying 6d. a day for each borrowed child; this was on a Thursday of the Whitsunday fair. She has been sometime in Glasgow, and now has a house in Jeffrey's Close, living with "Paddy Malone," a shallow lurker. They are both young people, and will no doubt produce a fresh cargo of beggars.

I crossed from Johnstone to Barrhead, and started in the morning to catch the breakfast hour at a bleachfield three miles on the road to Barrhead; here in a house I got upwards of a peck of meal. There were other three cadgers in the house, and they had got uncommonly large handfuls. I then proceeded about two miles further, where there was another bleachfield. I put off the time on the road, and went to that place at the dinner hour, and got another peck.

From thence I went to Barrhead, and stayed there a week. I "called" Hurlet and part of Barrhead; here I got nine tankards of meal and 6d. in coppers. Next day I "called" the remainder of Barrhead and Grahamston, where I had seven tankards and 2d. These two days, had I taken potatoes, I might have loaded a " cuddy."   Next day I went to Arthurlie and Gateside, where I took upwards of eight tankards, and next day went to Neilston.

I made several visits to other villages, and arrived in Stonehouse; this is an ordinary village, and filled with weavers, but here they do not suffer from depression of trade, as in large towns.   Every family has a garden, and has potatoes set with the neighbouring farmers.   I then turned to Larkhall, and turned out nine tankards of meal.   I then went to Hamilton and took lodgings, a small way in the town ; I think they call the place " The Back of the Barnes."

Hamilton is a long town containing a number of side lanes, and it took me three days to " call " it, but it is a dead town " considering."   There is little going for a strange cadger, as charity, here, goes mostly by the " kenned " face ; yet I believe it gives a deal of charity.   I have both cadged and cried this town before, and every time found it on the decline, but, on further looking into the matter I found a great number of Irish people settled here.   Their friends and acquaintances, calling on them, called also on their neighbours, and by degrees, made acquaintance with all in Hamilton who had anything to spare.

The first day I " called " the shops, and got the regular answer, " There is nothing for you to-day ; " after getting repeated answers to this effect, I determined to try if they were unanimous in their opinion, and next day tried the houses, but at many of them I got the answer, " We serve at the shop."   I was three days here, but I cannot boast of my good fortune.   I did better on any former occasion.   I cannot give the expense of the support of cadgers in this town.   There are a number of lodging houses that are in general well filled, but their number I did not ascertain.

From Hamilton I proceeded to Airdrie by Motherwell and Bellshill.   These villages are either very poor or have nothing to spare for the beggar ; and I came very poorly off till I arrived in Airdrie.   This town, I suppose, is the most thriving in Scotland, if not in Britain, and owes its prosperity to the minerals produced in the neighbourhood. This town and vicinity might be the seat of a troupe of cadgers, as there are villages all round which have " pays " every week ; this makes the money plentiful.

Miners are in general very free with what they have, and they are as well waited on. There are a number of hangers on, who take the different roads leading to Airdrie on the pay days. One of the times that I was there I saw a man, named Wilson, who lost his face by applying "scaldrums" in order to extract charity, and draw the pity of the public. He is well known all round the country, being blind, and using "scaldrums" on breast and arms. When sitting on the roadside he tells long "yarns," and quotes passages of Scripture in support of his beggary. He was, one Saturday, seated on the high road between Coatbridge and Airdrie, and that day he counted 22s., besides what he, and the woman who was with him, had drank.

This notorious old scoundrel was married to a decent woman, by whom he had a large family, some of whom are doing well. The respectable part of his family will not speak to him on account of his bad behaviour. After the death of his wife he got a young lassie to lead him, and the horrid characters were living as "man and wife" before she was fifteen years of age. She can now drink, and I can pledge her against any in Glasgow. I think at this time she may be about twenty-five, but the old debaucher does not even keep true to *her*.

He left Glasgow in May last, going to Edinburgh to get his "blue gown and badge" for begging, and left the young woman in a lodging-house in the Old Wynd. To see that good-looking young woman, not above twenty, one would have thought she would not have drank out of the same dish with him, but we must not always expect provident habits when we see a good-looking person and face. The young girl, with a child followed him to Edinburgh, and, when he understood she was in search of him, he returned to Glasgow ; *I* would blush to sit in their company.

This old man passes for a Scotsman, and, as appears on his badge, was bred to the sea, but was struck with lightning when on a voyage home from the West Indies. I have another account of him, from a person who knew him from a child ; that he is an Irishman by birth, and was never at sea ; but at an early period of his life, had committed a depredation for which he left the land of his nativity and started begging. In order to appear an object, he applied "scaldrums" to his body and face. By this means he has lost his eyes, and his body is marked in many places with the signs of his own horrid transactions. Within these thirty years, this person might have purchased an estate; whereas his bad behaviour has compelled him to beg from day to day.

There is also a blind young woman who frequented Glasgow and Airdrie, but being "overhauled," it was found that her father was a pensioner receiving 2s. 2d. a day, and, on receiving the pension they put it to a bad use ; by her begging, under pretence of being blind, they supported themselves, sitting on the bridges and roads round Glasgow. She was compelled to abandon the city for bad conduct, and was banished from Edinburgh before that, and is now living in Airdrie.

I could enumerate an incredible number that lurk constantly about Airdrie, and "can revel out life" in grand style by begging. A ballad singer can do well here ; "packman" begging is prohibited in the town of Airdrie, but, for miles round its villages, where public works are, the "pelfry" manufacturer does well, and is at no loss. There are a great number of lodging-houses in Airdrie, and their trade is good.

The two parishes of New and Old Monkland support daily upwards of one hundred vagrants. The expense of them I will put no name on, but an "acquaintance" of mine "calls" them often, and he informs me that he never "calls" the town of Airdrie (which he does by whining about the street with his hat in his hand), without receiving at the lowest 5s., and often 7s. As for me, I went far above that, but I had books, and told them tales.

I proceeded to Langloan, "calling" Coatbridge and Gartsherrie, and took 4s. 6d. besides paying for some drink, and lighted upon Cumbernauld. This is a poor town, and of small size ; I "cried " it, and what I received did not exceed 1s. ; I stayed there all night and went next day to Kilsyth. This town is a great seat of weavers, and is increasing, greatly owing to the different ores that are to be found in that neighbourhood.

There are five lodging-houses here, and one of them keeps nine beds; it is a great haunt of "delf" (stoneware) merchants. On account of the "waft" in this place, as in other manufacturing towns, they have "pops " (private pawnshops), that give advances on whatever is brought.

This is a system that ought to be spurned by every man of feeling, as it is the murderer of families, and gives the thief a double chance. When any article is sold to a broker, unless the broker be fully aware that the exposer is a thief, and the article stolen, it will be directly hung at the door for sale; while, in " pop," the article is concealed a month before exposure, and, when they know that it is not rightly come by, it is never seen at all. But as I am on my way to Glasgow, I will say no more about this till I reach it.

Kilsyth is only a town of working people, almost the whole of them in hardship, struggling through life; yet I have known one person, in one day, get five pecks of meal and a piece of salt beef that might weigh from eight to ten pounds. But this was not got by begging. The woman who had it was a "delf" and shoe merchant, but no doubt she made " a thief's bargain with a thief," whether it was from a wife, relation, or a servant, there is no doubt that it was a rogue's bargain; and, if it was not for " catches " of this kind, there would not be so many idle women running about with baskets.

Between the parish and the town of Kilsyth, I am within the number when I estimate the amount of beggars and hawkers of the different orders, at twenty each day. I will put no estimate on the expense of their support. I left Kilsyth and started for Campsie, and " called " the town; but like all other places of public works, when it was not the pay-day, pennies were scarce. I " called " it with books, but did little good, and I did not wish to cadge it, as I had acquaintances living there, and would not like to have taken their door.

Next night I stayed at the Milton of Campsie; I cadged it; it is but a small village, and I got four tankards of meal. I then started for Kirkintilloch; this is another den for travellers, as, from this place, they can take the villages of Gartshore, Chryston, Auchinleck, Torrance of Campsie, and Milton of Campsie; while the country round Kirkintilloch, any night, can turn out thirty vagrants on an hour's warning. This is a good country for gamblers and " bowl-hawkers." I will not lay an estimate on this place. I " cried " Kirkintilloch, but the book was of no use, as it was during the day when the people were all at their work. I did not take a shilling.

CHAPTER XII.

STREET ORATORY.

I STARTED for Glasgow, which I first saw, I think, in the year 1796 or 7, but, as a vagrant, I never appeared in it till the year 1818, on my return from England. I reached Glasgow on a Saturday in the month of November. My finances were small, and I did not wish to cadge in a place I was so well known. I was in a complete "habble;" a few pence was the amount of my fortune.

I had a woman with me who told me great things about her friends in Glasgow, being in good circumstances, and from whom she could get great things, but I placed no belief in her story, as I had heard so much of the boasting of travellers about their rich relations, and what they could do for them which never came to anything. We took lodgings in the "Flea Barracks" at the foot of the Old Wynd, kept by an Irish woman named Muir, who travelled and attended fairs to pass false money.

I went down to the street and saw an old man "calling" an eight-page book; I watched him, and he was selling tolerably well. I thought that, if he made a living by that, I would try and "breathe by the same air." I went to him and asked "where he got the books?" It was to Jamie Blue* I was speaking. His answer was, "D—l send you news."

At this time I knew nothing about books, nor where I could get them. I went up the Saltmarket, into a book-seller's shop of the name of Hutcheson, and asked "if he

---

* *Alias* "Blue Thumbs"—an old soldier named James M'Indoe, who was drummed out of the 71st Regiment to the "Rogues March"—a dealer in hardware, leeches, spurious pepper and blue; also a ballad singer and speech crier, one of the ne'er-do-weels of Glasgow. He died in 1837.—ED.

had any eight-page books for crying on the street?" He told me that "he had eight-page ballads, but no books." I asked the price, and he told me "twopence a dozen." I bought a dozen, and had laid out my little all, with only one penny behind. What was to be done? They were ballads, and I could not sing.

In this dilemma I stood for some time; had it been a strange town, it would not have cost me a thought, but it was Saturday night, and Sabbath day approaching. There was no time for deliberation, and to work I must go.

I would not appear in the Saltmarket, and proceeded to the Cross, and up the Gallowgate. In several places I made a stand, but could not think of beginning till I reached Calton Cross. By this time it was six at night. I then started, but looked at no one, lest I should be damped by seeing any person whom I knew.

What the ballads were I never knew, but at that time I had a grand voice, and gathered a crowd. I told them a long tale, as I found them totally in my hand. I held out the book, and in a few minutes I had sold the dozen. I returned and purchased three dozen, and went with them to the "Foot Barracks." I sold them in about half-an-hour, and returned again to the shop, where I purchased two quires; and was told that " if I wanted any more that night I would require to be there within half-an-hour, as they shut at eight o'clock."

I then "cast a gill in my neck," went to the Cross, and started. I was no time in drawing three shillings; I returned to the booksellers' and got other two quires, took another gill, and started again. I sold the whole by a little past nine o'clock and returned to the "Flea Barracks" where my wife was sitting in despair.

She had got 5s. from a friend, not expecting that I would have anything, but out of my twopence I brought home upwards of 6s. This was the first of my crying " specs; " I have continued at the trade ever since, and for long I spurned the name of a cadger. For many years this was a money-making business.

I soon got acquainted with some of the speech criers, and among the number was Jamie Blue, who took me to Thomas Duncan's printing office, in the Saltmarket. He kept a collection of the *best* old standard books of the "flying stationer" order in Scotland.   I selected those which were most likely to take the market.

An old copy of an eight-page book entitled "Willie Lawson's Courtship of Bess Gibb," was the first that I tried.   It was a peck of ill-put-together nonsense, but I afterwards found that *nonsense* was the article that "took" best in the street.   Of this piece I sold a number of reams, and cleaned out the shop ; I have never seen it since, and it is a small loss to the public.

I then chose another eight-page book called the "Haveral Wives," and sold a great number.   I had it reprinted at different times.   It was when "pattering" this book, that the women first marked me out as their enemy.

I "pattered" another called "John Thomson's Man," but, on account of some rude terms, which I knew would be improper to express in the street, I never used it ; still it reached the authorities, and I was taken to the police office, and prohibited from "calling" it any more.   I then fell in with "Janet Clinkers Oration on the Wit of the Old Wives, and the Pride of the Young Women."   This piece never fails.   I have turned it "heels over head" many times, and, when it would sell no longer, I gave it a fresh name, as well as a new introduction, and sold it as freely as ever.   In Edinburgh alone, the printer counted fifteen reams of it, and "Simple John," which I sold for my own hand, mostly at a penny each.   I changed its title to "Grannie M'Nab's Lecture on the Women," and sold it through the West of Scotland.

I then drew up "The Prophecies of 'Hawkie ;' A Cow," who prophesied in Fife, of a Prophet who appeared in Glasgow and converted numbers.   Like the *hand bills*, some bought them for fun, others out of contempt for the Prophet.

The prophecies of the cow "Hawkie" so exasperated the Glasgow Prophet, whose name was Ross—by trade a weaver—that one night as I was calling the prophecies of "Hawkie" in the Calton, where Ross resided, he attacked me like a madman, and had it not been for the people in the street I would have suffered persecution (like the rest of the prophets) from the hands of Ross.

By this book I got the name of "Hawkie," which has from that time stuck to me.   I "called" this book first in Glasgow, where every person knew the meaning of it; but when I went to Edinburgh and "cried" it, they did not know its meaning, and not knowing my name they called me "Hawkie" after the book.

One night, when sitting at the fire in my lodgings in the Old Wynd, Glasgow, a person related a story of an exciseman, who, when drunk, was found lying asleep by colliers; they took him down the pit along with them, and laid him in a corner; when he awoke he considered that he had died drunk and awaked in another world (?).

On hearing this tale, "Jamie Blue" interrogated the colliers, and their answers made him consider that this story would make a fine "patter." He observed to me "that he would have it written," but this, like the rest of Jamie's pretences, was never realised. A few days after, I asked Jamie if he intended to draw out a copy of "THE GAUGER," and he said "No !"

At that time I did not know that he had never learned to write. I told him I would do it myself, and next day I drew it out and gave it the title of "The GAUGER's Journey to the land of Darkness, what he discovered there, and his journey back."

When done I read it to Jamie, who thought that it would do well. He considered that it would not be safe to commit the printing of it to Mr Duncan, as he would give it to others as fast as to us; so he took me to one Ebenezer Millar, in the Saltmarket, where we ordered it to be printed under the condition that it was not to be sold to any other body, except by our permission. This he promised to do, and to have it ready next day. Next day, however, he went to the fishing, and we did not see him for three weeks.

At that time there was a man named Robertson under sentence of death in Glasgow, for housebreaking and theft, and the execution, which took place, 7th April 1819, brought "flying stationers" from every quarter. Jamie and I were "pattering" the "Gauger" before the execution. The strange "patterers" got copies, and it was soon in every town in Scotland, so that, although I had drawn out the speech and got it restricted, Jamie and I got very little good of it. There were only a few reams of it sold in Glasgow and Paisley, but I afterwards found a copy in Newcastle, turned into a song

and sung by a blind ballad singer, who really kept closer to
the original than the most of *clergy* do to their *text*.

The day before Robertson's execution Jamie and I were in
Wilson Street, and in a bookseller's shop saw a tract entitled
" A Reprieve from the Punishment of Death." As a reprieve
was expected for Robertson, we considered that this tract
was likely to sell.

We asked the price and were told " three half-pence." We
took four dozen each, and started ; Jamie in the Candleriggs,
and I in Bell's Wynd. I had scarcely reached Albion Street
before I had sold the four dozen, and turning back for more,
I met Jamie, who had sold about three dozen. On the head
of our good luck we proposed a " dram," to which Jamie
agreed, on condition that we would go to one Miller's cellar
in the Saltmarket.

I would not consent to this, as it was too far, and we might
be dogged by other speech criers, who would find out the shop
where we got the tracts ; but Jamie, who was naturally of a
cringing disposition, would go there, as they had given him
a dram in the morning, *on pledging his spectacles.* We went,
got the glass, and started again ; at night I had nine shillings.

Next morning we started it again, although the apparatus
of death was now fixed in front of the jail. We continued
pattering the " reprieve " till one o'clock, when the people
were collecting for the execution. By this time we were both
drunk, and had come as far as " The Cross." Jamie " took "
down the High Street, and I the Saltmarket.

I had not gone far when a boy came and told me to "stop,
as Jamie had been taken to the police office." A policeman
came down the Saltmarket, and I was sure he was in search
of me, but, at that time there were no less than seven speech
criers who used stilts, and not being so well-known I escaped.
I went to the printers to get some more books, and found
there dozens of speech criers, in as deep sorrow as if they had
been the friends of the unfortunate man, on account of being
prohibited crying the speeches, and thereby deprived of a
fuddle.

Thomas Duncan would sell none to be cried in Glasgow.
John Muir also printed speeches, and the criers went to him
to try and get some. When the criers left, Duncan told me
he would give me half-a-ream if I would go and sell them in

Paisley; I took them, and had got to the foot of the Salt-market when they were bringing the unfortunate man out to the scaffold. I went through the Briggate, started on the old bridge, and sold them all in one hour.

I could have sold more, but was afraid to go back as I had not kept my promise. I went to Muir's and got seven quires, intending to go to Paisley; but by this time Muir had sold his speeches, and the criers were out on the street.

When they began to cry, they were all apprehended and taken to " The Old Guard House " in Montrose Street, where upwards of fifty were kept over the Fast-day. Early on the Fast morning I went to the Guard House to see Jamie Blue, who was one of the unfortunates, and I handed him a gill through the window.

Jamie looked for nothing but " Bridewell " for crying the reprieve, and told me to keep out of the way. I went home and sent a woman with Jamie's breakfast, and started for Paisley. After I passed through Tradeston I changed my mind, and took the road by Renfrew for Greenock.

When I got to Renfrew there were two " patterers " there before me; when I saw them I was aware they were for Greenock also. A dram was proposed. They were as " kittle " neighbours as Glasgow could produce. One of them, William Anderson, had been three times transported for seven years; he and the other man, James Johnston, could never meet without a fight.

We got to Paisley and went into a public house. After drinking " half-mutchkins " (half an English pint) each, Johnston and Anderson quarrelled, and fought with their staves; they broke a number of articles in the room. Anderson got Johnston down, and when down, put Johnston's books in the fire, and held him till they were burned. Johnston got an opportunity, and burned Anderson's books.

The house was in danger of being burned, and the land-lord sent us to the black hole; they kept us there till next day, and put us out of the town. I still had my books, and promised to divide them when we were half-way from Paisley, at a place called " The Whiskey Well," where we proposed a gill, and went in; before we came out, my books were also burned, and we were all without a book. I was still in possession of a few shillings, and I was aware they were determined to make me spend the last farthing.

We came again to Paisley, and my two old boys cast out in the street, and were both taken to the Police Office. I was then rid of my neighbours, with whom I never thought to part till I had got a broken head.

I went to the house of George Caldwell, senr., a book-seller, who had retired from business, and was living privately at the head of "Dyer's Wynd;" but still kept a few small books to serve hawkers. He had a copy of an eight-paged book of which he had some reams. It was called "The Life and Transactions with the Trial and Burning of Maggie Lang, The Cardonald Witch," who suffered in Paisley, being the last that suffered in Scotland as a witch.*

This book had a great sale; I cleaned his shop of every copy, and got another book called "The Life and Transactions with the Trial and Burning of Maggie Osborne, The Ayrshire Witch." Of this book I sold a ream in one day; one half in the butter Market in Ayr and the other at the Cross of Ayr, in front of the house where she lived.

The old wives and children give historical traditions of this house. Her "master" (Satan), being convinced of her heroism in his service, determined to show his respect for her.

One night he built her a house, which stands to this day at the Cross of Ayr; it is three stories high. The story goes that when the inhabitants of Ayr went to their beds one night there was not a stone on the ground; he went to a quarry, quarried a large stone, placed it on his "rumple," and, with a broomstick between his legs, made his way through the air, and left it where the house now stands.

When finished with his complement of stones, he got lime and proceeded to the masonry, and by the crowing of the cock next morning, the house was completed. He was quarryman, carrier, barrow-man, and mason, and had Maggie in her own house by sunrise. I sold a number of reams of "Maggie" in Ayr.

* "Hawkie" is wrong here. Maggie Lang was the last witch burnt at Paisley; this occurred in 1697. But the last person actually burned for witchcraft in Scotland, was an old woman at Dornoch, 1722.

I also had a book called "The History of the Monastery of Crossraguel, in Carrick," twelve miles from Ayr. This monastery was burned by John Knox (who is said to have been himself an inmate of Crossraguel), and is now a heap of ruins. It says a great deal for the founder of the Presbyterian religion, that John Knox, in his zeal, vented his spite against stone and lime.

I was one night in the streets of Ayr when a gentleman spoke to me, and asked if I would take a dram with him. We went to a public house, and he asked me "if I could get books printed?" I told him "except for blasphemy and treason, I could get anything printed." He gave me a manuscript, containing seventy-four pages, and said "that it was his own production, and that as the case referred to himself, he wished to have it published, but did not want to do it himself."

I promised to look over it, and give him my opinion of it, and we appointed to meet two nights after. I read it carefully, and found it was a speech entitled "Honest Poverty in Distress, looking for a Friend." I brought it to Glasgow, and showed it to several people, and also to a gentleman by appearance, to whom I chanced to speak of it. He said he would like to see it, and would call at my lodgings for a sight of it. He called and got it away; I have never seen him since.

The next "patter" was "The adventures of Sandy in America;" of this I sold a great number; but it aroused jealousy between Jamie Blue and me, which only terminated at his death.

G

CHAPTER XIII.

"THE CROON O' THE CAUSEWAY."

JOHN MUIR, the printer, one day called at our lodgings, and told us he had a piece ready that only fitted Jamie and me. We went to his office, which was full of speech criers. I looked at the speech and saw that it would do, and Jamie, with a smile of satisfaction, said to me, "This will take the hill." I said that "I hoped it would, and I wished him luck of it."

From this remark, Jamie inferred that I did not intend to try it. He got a few beggars and Irish speech criers, strangers to Scotland, and its language—who could not read it, and hawked it through the shops. On his returning he ridiculed me for not countenancing it. I said that "if he had any respect for himself, he would not appear among a band of blockheads making fools of themselves."

Jamie's good sense made him ashamed to insult me when sober; but that period was only in the morning before he got on his clothes. I had to shun him on the streets as he would attack me. It was not Jamie's tongue alone; he had the reputation among the illiterate as a matchless scholar, and whenever he appeared on the street, a crowd always assembled, and anyone who contended with him was sure to lose, and receive the hisses of the crowd. I attempted to show Jamie that he had no claim as a scholar, but this only exasperated him the more.

One day in John Muir's printing-house, Jamie began boasting of his Scottish dialect, merely to vex me. I told him "he was a stranger to the Scottish dialect, and, if he would come out, I would give him a lesson." We agreed to have a trial of our abilities.

I urged the weakness of his ambition, and showed him

the meanness of his conduct; but Pompey was no more
determined for the Empire of Rome, than Jamie was to be
" Head speech crier." I requested him to make choice of a
book, and I would choose another. Jamie chose " Watty
and Meg," thinking that I would have no chance against
this, as that had been his hobby for twenty years. The
agreement was that the loser was to forfeit a bottle of
whisky. We were to start at the same time, with the same
quantity of books. The bookseller to give an account of the
numbers which each had received, and sold.

We started, Jamie choosing the Saltmarket and Gallowgate; and I taking the High Street and Trongate. Jamie
depended on groups of masons and labourers, who haunted
the head of the Saltmarket on winter nights.

I had " Watty and Meg " by heart from my infancy, but
how to " patter " it I knew not. Before going to my station
I turned back to Jamie's stance, and stood where I could
catch his voice, and one or two of his observations. I returned to the Cross, and, after two or three minutes study,
I started and held forth in the character of " A Cure for Ill
Wives."

I spun out a long yarn, and it was no time till I sold my
books, and returned for more. I went to the same place
where I had started, and raised the price to a penny, which
did not damp the sale. I sold a quire and a half, and returned for more. Jamie had never been in yet; he had only
half a quire at first. I sold what I had and went home, as
the hour for returning was ten o'clock at night. I was in
long before the hour.

When Jamie returned we counted before witnesses. Jamie
had one shilling and fourpence. I had nearly as many
shillings as he had pence. We drank the pledge, and Jamie
gave up the contest; but, when drunk, Jamie abused me,
and always showed a grudge. Since that time " Watty and
Meg " has brought me many a pound.

My next publication was in Edinburgh. A report spread
in town and country that a man, dressed in a bullock's skin,
with the horns fastened on his forehead, had robbed the
house of a maiden lady, under the character of " Auld
Clootie," compelling her to give up her goods, or be carried
off by him. A rumour was circulated of his apprehension

and trial, and that he had been sentenced to stand in the pillory in the High Street of Edinburgh on a day specified.

The day came, and the streets were teeming with crowds at an early hour in the morning, to get a sight of his horned majesty in affliction. I drew out the account of the apprehension and trial of " HAIRIE's COUNTERFEIT," and we hurried out to the streets, stating that the day of his punishment was that day fortnight.

Robert Menzies, in the Lawnmarket, who printed it, acknowledged that he sold six reams of the book that night, besides keeping his press going on it for three weeks.

I next published for a " Crispin " procession in Edinburgh the account of the " Ancient King Crispin " (patron saint of the shoemakers), in twelve pages of six-line poetry, but Menzies and I quarrelled about it. We brought it out, however, the day before the procession. I prohibited the printer from putting his name on the title page, for the criers not to find out where to get it.

I went out, and started opposite Bank Street. I was getting twopence a copy, as fast as I could take in the money, for about an hour ; when, on a sudden, the sale stopped, and I saw persons passing with copies in their hands. I turned round, and saw three criers selling them at the half of what I was crying. I put my books in my pocket, and went to remonstrate with the printer. He said, " He could not help it."

I was aware that other's money was as good to him as mine was, but it was never to their brains he applied for something that was needed. I took no more books from him, but went to Mr Glass, on the South Bridge. This circumstance brought Mr Menzies ten pounds that day, and the day of the procession ; but Mr Menzies conceded too much afterwards to the criers, and he ultimately lost by them.

I did not enter Mr Menzies' door for six months after that, not that I had a spite against him, because he was of a discreet and gentlemanly turn.

Mr Menzies and I afterwards came to an understanding : and I next sold for him a piece called, " The Adventures of a Temperance Gentleman from Edinburgh to Lasswade, on his horse 'GLANDERS,' being a Coffee-drinking Excursion." This piece consisted of forty-eight pages, and it sold well, but the friends of the gentleman paid me to stop it.

I next sold, for a newspaper office, a piece entitled, "The Expiring Groans, Death, and Funeral Procession of the *Beacon* Newspaper." This was printed on a sheet both long and broad, and sold at sixpence a copy. It sold well, one person taking a dozen at a time.

I was next employed by the masons, wrights, and plasterers of Edinburgh, to publish something against the masters, who had reduced their wages to 8s. a week that winter.

A number of delegates from each of the three trades waited on me, in a spirit cellar in the West Bow, on the Monday of "Hallow Fair," I think of 1826 or '27; and it was resolved to meet the next day on the Calton Hill, to make a full investigation into the case.

We accordingly met, and an effigy of the oppressor was brought out. A court sat, the panel was placed at the bar, and charged with breaking tradesmens' wages, found guilty by the jury, and sentenced to death. The procession then moved along Great London Street to the place of execution, before a builder's door, where the effigy was publicly burned.

At this time two men were sentenced to be hanged on Leith Sands, for piracy and murder at sea. The night *before* the execution, the criers were supplied with the last speeches of the condemned men. That night, having sold off all I had, I crossed the Mound to Princes Street, got another supply, and started at the end of the North Bridge; and, by the time I came in front of the Police Office, I had very few left.

I was taken into the office, and asked, What I had been selling? I said, "I was selling the speech of the men who were to be executed to-morrow, as there would be no more account to-morrow than there is to-day." This was the second and last speech of any unfortunate person that ever I "called."

My next effort was "STRAW" selling, and giving the book into the bargain, saying, "This is a most particular book, but I daurna' cry the book; 'deed, I daurna' either name the book, nor sell the book, but I will sell ony o' ye a *straw*, an' gie ye the book into the bargain." This "system" was new in Edinburgh, and I took money fast; the book I sold in this way was entitled, "Gilderoy, the Scotch Robber," of which I sold nearly twenty reams.

I returned to Glasgow, but did not now reside in "The Flea Barracks," with Mrs Muir, but lodged with William Bucklie, second close above St. Andrew Street. This man, although stout, young, and healthy, would not work, and started a lodging-house. He let four beds, which paid his rent and kept the family.

His brother was one of the lodgers, and hated work as much as he did; and, as it was winter, and snow on the ground, he had good reason for his conduct. Another of the lodgers was a silly young woman, whom they married to the brother, who meant to work after the New Year; and this poor silly creature begged for him for about nine months. He went to the Lothians, and, on his return, went to Ireland, where he had a wife, leaving the silly creature at the down-lying.

A man lodged in the house named O'Docharty. He was stout and healthy, but as unwilling to work as the others. He went about with a basket on his arm. I never found his stock to be worth half-a-crown. When a cadger came in with any cash or good luck, he would bewail his unfortunate state, and say, "It was my wife that was the 'getter;' she had a 'wheen' (several) houses she went to. They kept all for her, and she filled all the dishes when she returned. We had to go aside and take our victuals, that the rest of the 'workers' might not see the beef and fowls we had. But the devil tempted her to leave me."

When Billie Bucklie began the lodging-house business he kept boys, and afterwards arrived at the dignity of a "cuddy," and after that a horse, selling coals through the streets.

I next lodged in the New Vennel, and the first night I was there a man and woman came asking for a bed. They were admitted; and, after paying for their snooze, were accepted, and sent to lie with me. The man objected, and wanted back his money, but this was out of the question. They came to high words, and the man was driven out of the house. I fell asleep, and on waking I found myself hampered, and asked, How many were in the bed? when a woman answered, "There are three besides you." This is the third lodging in all my travels where they laid women in a bed with men. The other two were in Yorkshire.

I next lodged in Billy Toye's, in the entry from the Old Wynd to Jeffrey's Close. This fellow was a widower. His beds were all of one cast, and his demands were from two-pence to fourpence a night. I lodged in Billie's upwards of two years. Billie's "hotel" consisted of nineteen "snoozes," and a table which cost him sixpence at a roup. The house rent was about £6 or £7 a year.

We often counted Billie's income, and it was ten shillings a night for beds, besides other chances. When he first came to the Wynd he let only three beds; but, finding his trade increasing, and being unable to increase his premises, he raised one bed on the top of another; but this was not enough to satisfy his greed, and he decided to remove to more com-modious premises.

Billie, however, was an honest man, and would let nothing improper be done on his premises. When a woman and a man asked a bed, Billie told them " they might go to bed when they chose," but, as soon as they were ready, Billie shewed the man where to sleep with another man, and the woman with another woman.

Billie's Hotel was haunted with great legions of rats; it had hundreds of doors by which they could pass in and out. He pur-chased a large chest, to hold the lodgers' meat, as his door was open all hours of the night, and "troops" constantly coming and going; and as the person on duty through the night was some-times asleep, the meat was often stolen.

Billie asked me if I would take my bed on the chest to pre-vent the meat being stolen. I accepted the offer, as I had an opportunity of seeing the fun in the kitchen, and lay there about nine months; a box bed stood by the side of the chest and on it were put all the dirty dishes.

During the night, rats came by hundreds; as I lay on the chest forty or fifty rats would step from the bed-head on to my breast, and from that to the floor. They became uncommonly impudent.

One Sabbath morning, I was in the garret alone, and one of the lassies came carrying a plate, on which were bread, ham, and eggs, and placed the plate beside me. I considered it my duty to watch it lest any of the other women would come and steal it. In a short time a rat came and examined the articles on the plate; I lifted a "bauchle" (an old shoe) to cast

at it if it attempted to carry anything off.   It was soon joined
by two others; two of the three mounted the plate, and
rolled the eggs on the floor.

One of them cast itself on its back, and the other two rolled
an egg on to the breast of the one that lay on the floor; it
rolled it to its chin, seized the egg with its forepaws, and held
it fast.

The others then rolled a second egg on its breast, it then
placed the first egg between its chin and the upper joints of
its forepaws; and with the under joints held the second egg;
while the other two rolled a third egg on to the breast of the
one lying on the floor; it lifted its tail and caught the end
of it in its mouth, which supplied a rest to hold on the "car-
riage."   The other two seized its ears and were in the act of
" trailing " the rat, when I cast the " bauchle " and they gave
up their prize and fled.   I was alone in the garret, and had
it been a " hanging " case the rats would never had been
charged with the crime; I would have suffered as the guilty
party.

Another case of rats' depredations took place during my stay
in Billie's.   One Alexander Cairns, son of a stabler, by mis-
guiding himself, brought on trouble that caused his death.
When very ill he applied to his mother for relief, which she
declined to give, having probably been often tried before.
He died on a Sabbath afternoon; a neighbour woman came in
with a sheet, and cast it over the bed on which the corpse lay.
There was no attention given to the dead body.   On Monday
I went a small way into the country, and returned at night
" half fou'; " being sleepy I went to the bed in the garret,
which was next snooze to the bed on which the corpse lay.
I fell asleep, and awoke as day was breaking, about three in
the morning, and turned round to the side where the corpse
lay, when, to my surprise, something was moving under the
sheet.   I was lying as we always do in lodging houses,
" stripped to the buff."

The whisky being still in my head, and having heard of
dead folks coming back, I drew my shirt to me; there were
none but myself in the garret, the most of those who were
down-stairs in the kitchen being so drunk that they were unable to rise off their seats.   I put on my shirt, and looked
again to the bed, lest my eyes had deceived me, and saw an

extraordinary stickling about the throat of the corpse. I drew the corner of the sheet off the face of the corpse, when a number of rats started out by the head of the bed.

The first thing that I saw was some of the bones shining as if polished with a sharp instrument. I looked no further but went down the ladder, and roused Billie Toye, who went for a *coffin*.

When we examined the body, we found, that besides the eyes, the throat was eaten, and the body all mangled. Billie could not get a coffin from "the Session," as he was known to be in good circumstances. That day and night we watched the body, and we had enough to do to keep the rats off it with a stick. Billie went to the man's mother, and tried her for a coffin, but with less feeling than an animal, she refused to give it. At last the corpse was carried on a hurley to the Police Office, and what became of it I never knew.

Another circumstance took place in Billie's; one of the City Porters, who had parted with his wife, came and lodged there; he took to his bed and lay for some time, but always made a shift to pay his bed. One night, however, he had not the price, and Billie came upstairs demanding payment; the dying man told him that "he had it not."

Billie told him "to get up and leave the house directly" —the man said "he could not," when Billie drew him from the bed, and "trailed" him to the head of the trap, in order to put him out at the door. The man being far gone with asthma, this unmerciful outrage caused him to die on the trap-head. His friends were sent for, and, although they would not give one penny to support him in his illness, dressed his corpse in a respectable manner, and for fear of the rats, got a coffin fully mounted, *but* the women *stripped* him twice before the funeral.

Another mishap happened while I was in Billie's, to an old lame man, named John Weir, a native of Mauchline in Ayrshire. He was one of the few who held the Scottish Badge (as a King's beggar or "bluegown ").

The Irish consider everything their lawful prey that belongs to beggary. At the present time the number of bluegowns is twenty-nine, and of that number twenty-five are Irish.

Weir wandered about the country. He was without power in one leg and hand, and about nine months before his death, he was supported by the parish of Mauchline. A gentleman (?) belonging to that parish made Billie's John's home, and from what Weir received from the parish, and what the gentleman gave him, he was kept in a decent manner.

One day Billie went to the carrier's quarters to get Weir's money, the carrier was gone and he returned without the cash. He told his wife that he " would get no money for John Weir for another fortnight ;" when she heard this she got into a passion, and said " that he should not sit in her corner and not pay."

She drew him from the fireside and dragged him to the door in order to cast him out, but with his whole hand, he seized the side of the door and held fast; she dashed him down on the step, and split open his knee.

He looked up in her face and said, " you have got me thus far but you will never see me out." That night both were taken ill and were lying dead in the house at one time ; thus it happened as he said, for she was buried on the Saturday, and he on the Sunday.

This is the treatment that may be expected in lodging houses. However long you may have stayed in them, if you fall behind of one penny, you are driven to the door, and used in the most inhuman manner. These most notorious charac- ters, lodging-house keepers, are suffered to take an old house, perhaps an old stable or condemned house ; they start a lodging-house, which, every second night, will return them their original outlay. Many private houses are taken on this footing, and as some of them invest in drink, riotous living is carried on.

CHAPTER XIV.

THE GLOAMIN'—"SOME HAINED RIG."

I LODGED in a house in the Old Wynd in the winter of 1837, which had three beds, and two make-shifts; these were let at 5d. apiece each night, which amounted to 2s. 1d. The landlord was a weaver, who sometimes wrought and sometimes cadged. He was a man in the prime of life, and had two dandy daughters who wrought at the steam looms, and made 18s. each in the fortnight. The wife purchased a great quantity of "waft" (woof) from a dealer who had to flee from Glasgow; to raise the money the landlady had to pledge both bed and body clothes.

That winter, the destitute received relief, and this needy landlady applied to the parish, who visited her house; and the apparent poverty, combined with her pitiful, but lying tale, caused them to give her relief to the value of 22s., besides coals. At the same time, I knew a poor widow woman who applied to the parish, they visited her house and found it clean and tidy; they saw a *looking-glass*, and considered, that a woman having such an article was not entitled to relief, when all that she had to depend on for supper was a few spindles of yarn from a weaver.

Another lodging-house, in Jeffrey's Close, was let weekly at fourteen-pence, and often had thirty lodgers. There was not a society in Glasgow that the keeper did not impose on, and was partner with others in the same game. I saw, on one Saturday night, seven pecks of meal brought into the house, which had been obtained by imposture.

An ELDER would call at the house, and inquire about the character of a person at the *landlady*, taking the greatest ROGUE of the two to be an honest woman, because she paid the rent to the landlord. But the truth is she never would have had a house nor paid the rent, but for her and her lodgers' impositions. They received the tickets for the meal from a bookseller's in Queen Street.

James Given, after keeping a lodging-house in Jeffrey's Close for four years, one night sold the effects of his house for *nine shillings*, and went to America, having the sum of £176 in his possession, besides paying the passage of himself, his wife, and a son. This sum was the produce of 9s. they came into Glasgow with.

Billy Toye, with a lodging-house, in nine years, retired from business, purchased a farm in Ireland (which he paid on the spot), returned to Glasgow, and, after ten at night, went to a man whom he knew had money, and offered to contract for the "goodwill" of the hotel and furniture. The person and he could not come to an agreement, as the man considered *twenty* shillings was the value, and Billy wanted thirty.

Billy started to displenish his house, and, next morning, between five and six o'clock, with the assistance of a cuddy and a cart, he had the whole on a steam vessel at the Broomielaw before eight o'clock. So Billy set out for Ireland with a full breeze, arriving at his farm, and in nine years, besides keeping his family, he saved between £400 and £500.

There are a great many "lurkers," who take these houses by the week, but have no regard to keeping them in order; gathering no articles to make the house comfortable, but with caution avoid this, exhibiting to every visitor the wretchedness of this abode, and, with deplorable lamentations, as they say themselves, arouse the sympathy of the charitable by their tales.

It may be said that these things are written by me out of a bad heart, but, I mention it with the best intentions. I do not deny that I have *often* imposed myself, although never on charitable institutions; and I was always sorry to see the impostor step forward, and, with a pretended tale of distress snatch the supply from the deserving, although silent, real object of charity.

I am aware that the authorities are taking steps against vagrancy, and it is *time* they did. During the last war, if a man listed, and was going abroad, his wife was permitted to go with him to the port from which he was to sail, and was allowed a pass to carry her back to the place she belonged to. This pass or " route " allowed them three halfpence a mile to the end of their journey, but, if they chose to be cunning, they could make it twice as much as the sum allowed.

Hundreds found it so lucrative that they found " routes " independent of government, and, for many years, made a good trade of it. At the end of the war, that trade was done, and many soldiers and sailors who were dismissed the service, when in want, took up with a " router," and were recommended to try a pass.

Some women took them as a make-shift in the absence of their husbands, and found them in " passes " also. One enticed another, and by improper association, brought so many children into the world, that they had to be trained up to the cadge, or some other unprincipled occupation. Besides, there was the multitude that arrived daily from Ireland, with no other intention but to beg ; these took the road from Port-Dundas to Glasgow, showing themselves as objects of charity, and at night could be seen fighting in a spirit-seller's ; and women, who pretended to be objects of charity during the day, were found prostitutes at night.

During the summer of 1840, a good-looking young man came from Ireland, he was about thirty-five years of age, and had a wife and four children. He got work at Dennyloan-head, the wife and children remained in Glasgow and cadged. She took the two youngest with her; the two elder ones went out with " spunks," and were tasked to bring in a shilling a day each. At night and morning the two eldest were busy making "spunks," and started about ten o'clock to their " shifts."

On the Saturdays the woman went through the shops, as a number of them serve on that day, and I have known her bring in two shillings in halfpennies, besides bread and flesh. About four in the afternoon, on the Saturday, she went to the Cowcaddens as a beggar in general, and could bring home, by eleven o'clock at night from 4s. to 5s., but on the " big pay " sometimes 7s. and 8s.

The husband came every fortnight to see them, and, in place of assisting them, the wife could give him as much as 10s.; he had 18s. a-week, and, in May, had left a farm in

Ireland with victual and potatoes in the ground, four cows to be milked, and a horse to be wrought by a neighbour, to be accounted for to them on their return at Hallowmas. I read the letters from Ireland, stating the account of the crop and cattle.

If the husband had had the spirit of a "flea," and if the woman had had a conscience, they would have been ashamed of themselves when begging; but a beggar needs no conscience, and if they have one, they must not use it, for by so doing, they will murder their profession.

It is true that begging is an honest shift for a poor old man or woman, or for a person deprived of their reason, or deprived of the use of their limbs; and to prosecute them would be a dangerous step; but for children to beg is a crime against the law of the country. If the parents are unable to provide for them, they should be looked after by the parish; but, if the parents are in health, they must be compelled to provide for their children.

If the parents are out of work, and if necessity demands begging, let the parents do it; as the child that is bred to begging seldom settles to an honest employment. Besides, it encourages a spirit of meanness and covetousness. There are a number of excuses for begging by persons who are not proper objects. Those lame of a leg, and deaf, and dumb, could find employment to suit them if they were possessed of their faculties in their youth.

A number of worthless parents take advantage of children who are disabled, and send them to beg, because they know that their youth will draw the charity of the public, and they are quite regardless of the child's fortune in life. They are thus doomed to perpetual beggary,—almost the lowest of all low professions. The poverty of the country, and the want of law, first gave beggars countenance; but I believe none practised it who could make a better shift. In begging, as in everything else, greed and disreputable idle-set increased the number, and generation after generation swelled it, till, by their impositions, the country has got tired of them.

During my stay in Glasgow I got Bridewell four times— sixty days each time. This I got as a reward for drunkenness, yet I still took a "drap," and persisted in it, till it has more than once brought me to the jaws of death.

I have been three times in the Town Hospital in Glasgow, and I consider it to be the best hospital in Scotland, and excelled by few in England. I have been in different hospitals in England—in some for a night, and in others longer. I was in the hospital of Belford, and in that of Bedlington, in Northumberland.

I was six weeks in the hospital of South Shields, in Durham, having inflammation of the bowels; the hospital was superintended by a man named Hunter. The inhabitants of South Shields showed the utmost kindness to me. They lifted me off the street, and with great care conveyed me to the hospital, where the doctor used his utmost skill.

The superintendent, however, appeared to be of a different stamp; his name was Hunter, and, when I was recovering, the doctor ordered me extra diet, but Hunter paid little attention to his order, and, save one meal, I got always the house allowance, which was a pint-tin nearly full of something they called "boilies;" it was made of oatmeal, but was neither gruel nor "stirabout." I think that an ounce and a half of meal formed the composition, with milk, morning and evening.

For dinner, on Sundays, we got a little pea-soup, containing mint, seasoned with pepper, about half a mutchkin; a slice of loaf—perhaps three ounces—and a small piece of meat. Two days in the week we got potatoes and herring; on other days about six ordinary potatoes, and nothing else. Two other days we had a pudding, which was considered extra, but I saw nothing extra about it, as it seemed to be made of flour, a little kitchen-fee, and a small *acknowledgment* of molasses.

I was also in the hospitals of Scarborough and Hull, in Yorkshire; I was one night in the one, and from Saturday till Monday in the other, to both of these hospitals I am under the greatest obligation; yet let the truth be told, the Glasgow hospital is the best, and the manner in which it is conducted I will here faithfully give.

The house consists of near five hundred inmates, and is managed by a committee selected from the different trades and merchants of the city. To this committee is entrusted the management, not only of the inmates of the hospital, but also out-pensioners.

The hospital is conducted by a governor, and clerk, who conduct the business both within and without the house. A matron to whose care is committed the whole of the cooking for the inmates, and the laundry, as also the superintending of the nurses of the different wards ; and to see that the lunatics are properly attended to, and those who are in the sick room. A doctor is also in the establishment. And a chaplain to attend to the moral and spiritual wants of the inmates. Besides the porter, the hall-keeper, and his substitutes are inmates of the hospital—a shoemaker with substitutes—a tailor with substitutes.

The house is supplied with victuals of the best quality. The clothing is comfortable, and, although strong, not coarse ; neither is the colour and make of a forbidding distinction. The inmates are provided with shoes and stockings, and a shirt and neckcloth—changed weekly. The beds are truly comfortable. The wards of the inmates are washed twice a week, under the superintendence of the nurse of the ward. The rooms are all well provided with fire.

The inmates who are in good health, get about two pints of substantial well-made porridge, of the best grain, with an imperial half-mutchkin of milk for breakfast ; each day for dinner, the same quantity of good broth, full of barley and vegetables, with either oaten or flour bread.

" When badly, diet and cordials are ordered by the " directions of the house-surgon, and the given out comited " to the matron. The hospital is blised with a matron of simpo- " thetick feeling, and attends mor to comforts of the distrest " than the former matron. The supper of the inmeats is the " same as brakefast—in trwth, the whole stwddies to the " utemost the comfort of the inmeats ; there's few yowths as " it is considered proudent to bord them in the different " directions of the country, least by having them together, " vises might be introduced.

" I consider it prowdent at this time, to end my peri- " grinations hear."

(The above paragraph is an exact copy of the original spelling, &c.)

APPENDIX.

—•◆•—

THE preceding pages exhaust Hawkie's Autobiography; there are other leaves among the manuscripts which are either written in a different hand, or, for other reasons, do not appear to be genuine, but there are many letters, addressed to Mr David Robertson, Bookseller, Trongate, Glasgow, which have the " pure ring " of Hawkie about them. From those the following selections have been made ; the prominent feature throughout many of them seems to be the want of his dearly-loved tobacco, which, next to whisky, was Hawkie's favourite " weakness." He did not *smoke* much, although, in one letter, he writes, " And send it round for smoking." This may have been to oblige a brother in distress, although it is difficult to conceive many, or even any, facilities for smoking in an hospital. Hawkie's way of using the " weed " was " chewing," and he never wanted a " quid " when he could get it.

Most of the letters bear that they came from the " Town's Hospital," Glasgow ; some do not indicate from whence they came, but, from reference to " spells " at the " Oakum " it may be inferred, that they were written in places where stricter rules prevailed, and from page 110 it may be presumed that they came from " A Government Temperance Hotel," although these were much laxer in discipline in former days than they are now.

Many of the letters bear no date, and it is difficult to arrange them in chronological order. Being an Autobiography, it would be quite apart from the plan of the book to supplement its graphic pages by any imported matter; suffice it to add, that Hawkie died in the City Poorhouse, Parliamentary Road, Glasgow, September 1851, DEEPLY REGRETTED, and that by many he is still "fondly remembered."

The letters are copied *verbatim*, and might be enlarged upon as establishing Hawkie's claim to be one of the forerunners of the reform of the English language known now-a-days as "Phonetic Writing."—Let them speak for themselves.

On March 15th, 1842, he writes from Town's Hospital, Glasgow, to Mr David Robertson, Bookseller, Trongate, Glasgow :—

SIR,
I am sory to state that I only on Tewsday last received the glasses from Mr Muier, and a bad fit ; however I wil make them do and I have no tabel, and has to stand and writ on *the foot* (sic.) That disconvenience arises from Mrs Reid's mother being badely this some time, and is at presant lying a corp. I hear to be intered on Munday. I think if you would send a line to Mr Stirling he would find me a table,
Sir I remain to Be yower,
Servant, WILLIAM CAMERON.

And he adds the following pathetic, poetical, single stanza, "so sad, so true."—

P.S.—No farther with my pen a'l win (I'll get)
Take pity on a pip that's time (empty)
For ardent spirits this place keeps free
Tea tottels home, let its name be !

(Eh ! but I'm dry ! dry !! ED.)

To THE SAME.

SIR,
I received youer card with the tobaco for which to you I wil consider myself for ever indetted ! in youer card you request a gloasery on the cant. Were a glosary not given the cant would then be a dead langwage, and could I not define it I would prove a fool to myself

and an imposter on you, which is avers to my natural principals however corupted. I wil give you a corect translation of every cant term used by me in the narative, and for the narative, if I go beyond truth I am aware that it would mak me the loast character in existance, as every town and village in my perigreenations can judge for itself as for what has taken pleas between me and my congregations on the street. I am in general drunk when they happen and I do not commit them to memory. Sir, I do not wish to be greedy but a bit tobaco would be aceptibal—

Sir with all due respect

and send it   I remain
    round   Your humble Servant
for smoking.   WILLIAM CAMERON.

Mr David Robertson, Bookseller, Trongat, Glasgow.

TO THE SAME.

SIR,

A disagreable needsesity urges this intrusion. I should not wish that a steatment of my presant circumstances should cast you into the despond in which I am pleast. My possions (possessions) at present consists of a steedy (steady) hand, a geasend (very, very, parched) throat a dry heart, and an empty pip (pipe). I have heard people prayed for in kirks with les than half the troubls, but, ye ken, I was alyes unwilling to tell the publick of my poverty. (*Eh Hawkie ! Hawkie !—Editor*) and if you would be so good as smudder (smother) the report with a morsel of tobaco, youer humble servant, and afflicted petitioner, as in duty bound shall ever pray.

N.B.—I have now theierty (30) subjects new to the woreld but I have only compleated theierteen page of peaper, as my dask is the bottom of a window and writes standing on the *left foot*.

I am Sir
with all due Respect
yowers

WILLIAM CAMERON.

NOTE.—Hawkie had no other foot *to stand on.* (ED.)

TO THE SAME.

SIR,

My mind is made up not to be long in this Garison, although I have no reluctance at the Billet. The waather is setting in favourabel. I am a bird of, and inclins the open air, and inclined to chirm in the open air, however I am a mind to continue another fortnight. I have now theierty-six subjects new to the woreld among which are a sceach (sketch) of the life and adventers of Andrew Wood, Daft Dawson of

Menstry, a blink il (?) eye, a charm for the toothaik by a tailor with his wonderful adventers, Billey O'Neals steatment of the differance between hanging in Scotland and Ireland, with the life and adventers of James Cock-up as a Unitarian Exorter with his defenses at the police Court. I would not wish to break you, but, if you would be so kind as send me a bit tobaco it wil be thankefulley received.

Sir

I am with all due respect

Youers

WILLIAM CAMERON.

The reference to Oakum in the following letter, makes one wonder (?) *where* Hawkie *lodged* at the time,—

Sir,

The card that you sent along with the scroal I droped what it conteand, I know not if it conteand any particwlars; pleas send a not of it with the Bearer. I have to attend the oakem from ten til wan fornoon, and from three till five afternoon, so my time to writ is scanty. I am dying for tobaco, if it wowld come up yower bak to send me a smak it wowld releeve the drooping spirits of

Sir,

Yower Humble and unfortunate

W. CAMERON.

N.B.—Since twesday I have feild eight page.

And, again, Tobacco is the theme—

Respected Sir,

In order to prevent defrawd, I send you thes lines steating a most lamentable teal and sorrey to add too trew—I am out of tobaco, has no money, creadet crackt, and accounts due that makes me keep under cover; and even from my residence breathes out the yewls (yowls) of cadging and hopping the cry will penetreat yower ears and touch yower heart. Ower governor is truely bad for which I am seriousely sory, as I am aware, was this house to loas (lose) him, they would loas a sensear friend, and the towen an honest man. I do not expect a sealebele news peapre, but be so kind as send me an old wan of some kind.

No more, But remains

Sir, unfortenat HAWKIE.

Glasgow Town's Hospital,   Pleas return with
    Febv. 16—1847.   the Bearer.

The following long epistle is in Hawkie's best style, and the "medicine" ordered for him must have been *greatly to his mind*—

Sir,

When a person strays from hom and enters a foraen clemet, after staying sometime, he, in general, sends back a letter giving his opinion of his new residenc, giving a steatment of its inhabitance with their customs and maners both sivel and religeous, with the produce of the country together with the trowbels that naterly ariseth in the clemit. The inhabetens are devided into three secks—wan seck are embesiles or lunetecs, another leam (lame) or deseased, woren out, men and weamen, whos circumstances in life has compeld them to become papers (paupers), a third and most notorious are a mixter of notorious drunkards, the ban of morality, the offscourens of brothels, fling out of bredwals (Bridewells) the refuse of Bottany bay (*an early penal settlement—Ed.*), so that in this colny there is a diverity of spirits as wel as sitewations of distresses, so that, although we are don to far beyond what we deserve, yet the discutions that ariseth among the lawles, unruly, tribe holds this place in as much agitation as Danl O'Conel did the Parliment. Yet, I confes in concience, that like all other evils, our unhapieness arises from ourselves.

I have been wors at this time that at any time I viseted the Hospital. I am indetted in a particular maner, to Dr Dick for his attention to me. The governor and matron acts towards the inmeats in such a parentle maner that decleares them worthy of the charge comitted to them. Our cheplen, I consider, is a Christian and wisheth well both to souel and body of the inmeats and would fain gather them as a hen gathereth her chicans under her wing, but ther is a number of us lik the Jews, pron upon our idols and after them we go. This place speaks in high creadit to the town of Glasgow as it is the secret closet for the eadged (aged) to make up their minds for an everlasting hom, a bed of downs for the aflicted, a creadle for the outcast infent, and a nurs for the parenteles orfint, and a city of refuge for the self-destroyer. Although I have no cause to complain as my coch (cough) is lifted and the asmy (asthma) is in a great maner removed. I am timerous about changing my billet for a few weeks longer, as I am not keen of the snows of February and the winds in March; yet, or ever it go far in March, if I be speared in health earely in March, I will expereance the sweets of the Spring, if not on wings, on stilts.

They are preparing the Garden, but they tell me that "it is too much inclind to the North Pol to grow TOBACOA. Give my compliments to Docter Graham, and tel him that, in sinserity I wish him plenty of work and good payments at whosever's expenses : and as you are in the book way, if you would get a cal for the "*Aflicted Man's Companion*," I can ashor you that you can be supplied with some hundreds of copies of the first quality, at greately redust prises, in Bridgate and Old Wynd. As I am very anchious to know how "Dan" is coming on with the "Repeil" rent, if you have a newspaper to spear, and would give me a reading of it, I would take it kind.

I am breaking out in boils, Doctor Dick alowes it is the poverty of my blood and allowes me a glas of whisky every night. I am quite happey in my sitewation, though not altogether content. I must be thankeful for the appearing respit I have got, and considering I never was willing to doo mutch.

I therefor conclud,

Sir,

I remain in the town's Hospital, the Benefactor of you and every contributer for the Town's Hospital and other charitable instetution, and may yower temperals be returned seventy fold spiritwal, is the sinsaer prayer of yowers.

W. CAMERON.

APPENDIX No. II.

One of the best descriptions of Hawkie, as well as a genuine illustration of his style, is given by William Finlay, (one of the many geniuses that have sprung from Paisley), in his "STREET ORATORY." The piece has the additional advantage of having been considered by Hawkie's kindest friend, the late Mr David Robertson, already so often referred to in this work, as worthy of a place in his admirable collection of songs for the social circle "Whistle-Binkie." It embodies references to others of Hawkie's "*friends*," and is altogether so graphic, that the following long quotation from it may confidently be given as a fitting conclusion to this "Autobiography."

Finlay's description of Hawkie is as follows :—

"We suppose the name Hawkie was bestowed on our Trongate Demosthenes, on account of his manner of articulating ; a hawking-up-throat-sawing tones, as if there were a war in the windpipe, and the antagonist forces very nearly balanced :—were our orator, instead of rattling pebbles in his mouth, to modulate the tone, to try the friction of a bottle-brush in the passage, it were more likely to do good. This character must be known to most of our readers ; his real name is William Cameron. He may be seen, almost every night, in one or other of our principal streets, surrounded by a mob, haranguing them on the topics of the day.

Hawkie's readiness in repartee is truly astonishing—and woe betide any of our whiskered-cigar-smokers who attempt to break a lance with him! the coarse sarcasm with which he assails them is as easily borne as a ladleful of boiling pitch poured down the back. Hawkie is a very extensive Manufacturer of Facts ; with a most copious vocabulary, the warp and woof of his Munchausen fabrics, are of wonderful consistency. He is far superior in point of natural talent to what Jamie Blue was, even in his best days, between whom and Hawkie there existed a most jealous rivalry.

Jamie put in his claim as greatly Hawkie's superior in the Dialogue, indorsed with 'It's aboon his fit.' Hawkie, on the other hand, cut his rival as with a butcher's saw, telling him that he knew nothing of the language, that he addressed the public in, 'Come out to the street, and be a listener, and I'll let you hear the Scottish language in its pith and purity ; ye ken as muckle about it, as grumphy does about grammar.'"

And the pen-picture of the Glasgow streets and street-characters, which he gives in the following piece, will vividly recall to elderly readers the Glasgow of fifty to sixty years ago, as well as enable the present generation to realise what they have often heard their fathers and grandfathers relate with hearty glee.

STREET ORATORY.

AIR—"*Bartholomew Fair.*"

'Tis a most amusing sight,
For a philosophic wight,
Through the streets of the city to stroll—
And mark the variation
Of this mighty population,
As the great tide onward doth roll.

What a bustle, what a noise,
What variety of cries,
Every one tries another to out-bawl ;
You would think the Tower of Babel
Had again let loose its rabble,
Such a clatter ne'er was heard since the Fall !

What a comical compound,
And diversity of sound,
From the motley group doth arise,
From your salt and whit'ning venders,
Fiddle scrapers, organ grinders,
And your sellers of yard-long shoe ties !

See yonder crowd collected,
Every one with ears erected
Around the far-famed Jamie Blue ;
The affair, depend upon't
Of the which he gives account,
Is full, and particular, and true !

Blind Aleck next appears,
Whose head for many years,
A hot-bed of poesie has been ;
With his violin in hand,
He now takes up his stand,
And thus his harangue doth begin :—

. . . . . .

Thus ends Blind Aleck's song,
And from the list'ning throng,
A burst of applause is heard:
And the charitable section,
Of the crowd make a collection,
For the comfort of the poor blind bard.

So the comedy goes on,
And the characters each one,
Have their parts made exactly to fit.
But who, ye powers of mirth,
From the canvas next steps forth ?
'Tis Hawkie—the orator and wit.

CROAKING BARITONE—(*Anglice*—Barrowtone) OF VOICE.

"A-hey! bide a wee, bodies, and dinna hurry awa hame, till ye hear what I hae gotten to tell ye ; do you think that I cam' out at this time o' nicht to cry to the stane wa's o' the Brig'-gate for naething, or for onything else than for the public guid?—wearing my constitution down to rags, like the claes on my carcase, without even seeking a pension frae her Majesty ; though mony a poor beggar wi' a star o'er his breast, has gotten ane for far less."

(*Voice from the crowd*)—"Hawkie, ye should hae been sent to parliament, to croak there like some ither parliamentary puddocks till yer throat were cleared."

(*Reply*)—"Tak' aff your hat when ye speak to a gentleman—it's no the fashion in this kintra to put hats on cabbage stocks—a haggis would loup its lane for fricht afore ye—ye'll be a king whare a horn-spoon is the emblem of authority!" (*Resumes*)—"Here ye hae the history of a notorious beggar, the full and particular account of his birth and parentage—at least on the mither's side. This heir to the wallets was born in the byre of a kintra farmer, an' just in the crib afore the kye, and was welcomed to the world by the nose of honest Hawkie."

(*From the crowd*)—"Was this a sister of yours, Hawkie ?"

(*Answer*)—"Whatna kail yard cam' ye out o'? that's your brither aside ye, is't ? you're a seemly pair, as the cow said to her cloots."

(*Continues*)—"It ne'er could be precisely ascertained the hour o' this beggar's birth, though the parish records hae been riddled to get at the fact. I maun also tell ye, for I dinna like to impose on my custo-mers, that there is great doubt about the day o' the month, an' even about the month itsel'; but that he was born hasna been disputed, though it might hae been, if we hadna an account o' his life and death, to convince the gainsayers. He arrived sooner at the years o' discretion than usual; an' if ye dinna ken the period when a beggar's bairn comes to his estate duly qualified, I'll tell you—it's when he ceases to dis-tinguish between ither folk's property and his ain."

(*From the crowd*)—"What a poor stock ye maun hae; ye hae been yelling about that beggar, till the story is as bare as your ain bellows."

(*Retort*)—"Hech, man, but your witty—when ye set out on the tramp, dinna come to me for a certificate, for I really cou'dna recom-mend ye; ye havena brains for a beggar, and our funds are no in a condition to gi'e ony pensions the now." (*Continued*)—"Ye hae an account o' the education which he received riding across the meal pock; and the lair that he learnt aff the loofs o' his mither, which was a' the school craft he e'er received: but sic a proficient did he himsel' grow in loof lair, that, like a' weel trained bairns, he tried his hands on the haffits of his auld mither in turn, and gied her sic thunderin' lessons, that she gied up her breath and business in beg-ging, at the same time, to her hopeful son and successor."

(*Voice from the crowd*)—"Ye should hae keepit a school amang beggars, and micht hae ta'en your stilt for the taws."

(*Retort*)—"Oh, man, I would like ither materials to work wi' than the like o' you; it's ill to bring out what's no in; a leech would as soon tak' blood out o' my stilt, as bring ony mair out o' you than the spoon put in." (*Resumes*)—"Ye hae an account of his progress in life, after he began business on his ain account, and what a skilful tradesman he turn'd out—he could 'lay on the cadge'[1] better than ony walleteer that e'er coost a pock o'er his shouther."

"Ye hae an account o' his last illness and death—for beggars die as weel as ither folk, though seldom through a surfeit; ye hae also a copy of his last Will and Testament, bequeathing his fortune to be drunk at his dredgy—the best action he ever did in his life, and which mak's his memory a standing toast at a' beggars' carousals—whan they hae onything to drink it wi'; and really, you'll allow me to remark, if we had twa or three mae public-spirited beggars in our day that would do the like, the trade might yet be preserved in the country—for it has been threatening to leave us in baith Scotland and England, in consequence of the opening up of the trade wi' Ireland, and the prices hae been broken ever since; we hae a' this to contend wi' to preserve the pocks frae perishing, for the sake o' our children."

(*Voice from the crowd*)—"Och, Willie, is it your own self that I'm hearin' this morning? and how did ye get home last night, after drinking till the daylight wakened ye? troth ye did not know your own crutch from a cow's tail."

(*Retort*)—"Oh, man, Paddie, it's naething new to me to be drunk, but it's a great rarity to you—no for want o' will, but the bawbees. What way cam' ye here, Paddie? for ye had naething to pay for your passage; and your claes are no worth the thread and buttons that

[1] Skilful address in begging.—*Dict. of Buckish Slang.*

haud them thegither;—gin I had a crown for every road that your trotters could get into your trowsers by, it would be a fortune to me. 'Take me over,' said you, to your ould croak-in-the bog; —'I wish I had my body across agin, out of this starvation could country, for there's nothing but earth and stones for a poor man to feed on; and in my own country, I'll have the potatoe for the lifting.' Hech, man,—but the police keeps ye in order—and ye thought when ye cam' o'er, to live by lifting? man! aff wi' ye to your bogs—there's nae place like hame for ye, as the Deil said when he found himsel' in the Court o' Session."

" Ye hae an account o' this beggar's burial, and his dredgy."

(*Boy's voice from the crowd*)—"Was ye there, Hawkie? surely, if the stilt could haud ye up!"

" Och, sirs, are ye out already—you're afore your time—you should hae staid a wee langer in the nest till ye had gotten the feathers on ye, and then ye would hae been a goose worth the looking at."

(*Continues*)—"Sic a dredgy as this beggar had wad mak' our Lords o' Session lick their lips to hear tell o'—thae gentry come down among us like as mony pouther-monkeys—with their heads dipped in flour-pocks, to gie them the appearance o' what neither the school or experience in the world could teach them;—gin hangie would gie them a dip through his trap-door, and ding the dust aff their wigs— there's no a beggar frae John o' Groat's to the Mull o' Galloway, that wadna gie his stilts to help to mak a bonfire on the occasion.

" Ye hae the order o' the procession at the burial—it's the rank in the profession that entitles to tak' precedence at a beggar's burial—ye never hear tell o' blood relations claiming their right to be nearest the beggar's banes; we'll be thinking the warld is on its last legs, and like to throw aff its wallets too, when sic an event occurs."

(*Interrupted*)—"Your stilt would, nae doubt, be stumpin' at the head o' them a'."

(*Reply*)—"Stan' aside, lads, I'm just wantiu' to see if he has cloots on his trotters, for horns are sae common, now-a-days, amang the gentry o' the blood, whar we should look for an example, that they hae ceased to distinguish the class that nature intended them for."

(*Goes on*)—"First in order was Tinklers, the beggars' cavalry, wha being in constant consultation with the gentry of the lang lugs, hae some pretentions to wisdom; next Swindlers, wha mak' the best bargains they can wi' their customers, without pretendin' to hae ony authority for doin't—no like our black coats, wha can only get authority on ae side, to gang to a scene of mair extensive usefulness, whar the preaching pays better—our brethren of the pock a' follow this example; they never stay lang whar there's naething either to get or to tak',—but I'm forgetting mysel'; at their heels was Pickpockets, wha just tak' the hangman's helter wi' them, and gang the length o' their tether—for hangie aye keeps the hank in his ain hand."

" Next, Chain drappers—the jewellers in the camp, wha are ready to sell cheap, or half the profits wi' everybody they meet, and wha are like mony o' our public instructors—aye get mair than they gie—then Prick-the-loops, wha are sae familiar wi' the hangman's loop that they've turned the idea into business, and set up wi' their garter—

which they can easily spare, as they hae seldom ony stockings to tie on wi't : by this simple expedient they mak' large profits on sma' capital. Next, Chartered-beggars or Blue-gowns—wha get a license frae the authorities to cheat and lie over the whole country."

"Next, the hale clanjamfrey o' Vagrants—for they're a' but beggars' bairns the best o' them—Randies, Thieves, Big-beggars and Wee-beggars, Bane-gatherers and Rowley-powleys—Criers o' Hanging-speeches—wha, generally, should hae been the subject o' their ain story—some wi' weans, but a' wi' wallets, broken backs, half arms, and nae arms: some only wi' half an e'e—ithers wi' mair e'en than nature gied them—and that is an e'e after everything that they can mak' their ain ; snub-noses, cock-noses, slit-noses, and half-noses ; Roman noses, lang noses—some o' them like a chuckie-stane, ithers like a jarganell pear ; hawk-noses and goose-noses ; and mind ye, I dinna find fault with the last kind, for nature does naething in vain, and put it there to suit the head ; but whatever the size and description o' the neb, they could a' tak' their pick, for the hale concern, man and mither's son, had mouths, and whar teeth were wanting, the defect was mair than made up by desperate willin' gums."

"Some were lame, though their limbs were like ither folks ; there are mae stilts made than lame folk, for I maun tell ye some gang a-begging and forget their stilts, and hae to gang back for them afore they can come ony speed ; ithers had nae legs to be lame wi' ; a few like mysel' had only ae guid ane, like the goose in a frosty morning, but made up the loss by the beggars' locomotive, a stilt, which a poor goose canna handle wi' advantage.

"The rear o' this pock procession was closed by bands o' sweeps, wha are ready for a' handlings, whar there's onything to do for the teeth ; an' they hae the advantage o' us, for they'rs aye in Court-dress, and like honest Colly, dinna need to change their claes."

"In the hame-coming there was a scramble, wha should be soonest at the feast, and a quarrel, an' you'll maybe be surprised that there was but ae quarrel, but I maun tell you, that they were a' engaged in't, an' maist o' them kentna what they were getting their croons cloored for, but just to be neighbour-like. The cracking o' stilts, the yelly-hooings o' wives and weans, and the clatter o' tinkler's wives, wad hae ca'm'd the sea in the Bay of Biscay—do ye ken the distance at which a beggar fights his duel ?—it's just stilt-length, or nearer, if his enemy is no sae weel armed as himsel'.

"Ye hae a return o' the killed and wounded—four Blind Fiddlers with their noses broken—four Tinkler's wives with their tongues split, and if they had keepit them within their teeth, as a' wives' tongues should be, they would have been safe—there's nae souder or salve that can cure an ill tongue—five Croons crackit on the Outside—sixteen torn Lugs—four-and-twenty Noses laid down—four Left Hands with the thumb bitten aff—ten Mouths made mill doors o'—four dizen Stilts wanting the shouther-piece—twenty made down for the use of the family—in ither words, broken in twa ; an' they're usefu', for we have a' sizes o' beggars. After a' this, the grand dredgy ; but I havena time to tell you about it the night ; but ye see what handlings beggars would hae if the public would be liberal.

"Buy this book : if ye hae nae bawbees I'll len' ye, for I'm no caring about siller. I hae perish'd the pack already, an' I am gaun to tak' my Stilt the morn's morning, and let the Creditors tak' what they can get."

This is the end of all,
High and low, great and small ;
This finishes the poor vain show,
And the King, with all his pride,
In his life-time deified—
With the beggar is at last laid low.

WORKS BY THE EDITOR

Bits from Blinkbonny; or, Bell o' the Manse. A Tale of Scottish Village Life between 1841 and 1851. Thirteenth Edition. Crown 8vo, cloth, 2s. 6d.; cloth extra, with Six Original Illustrations, 3s. 6d.

More Bits from Blinkbonny. A Tale of Scottish Village Life between 1831 and 1841. Fifth Edition. Crown 8vo, cloth, 2s. 6d.; cloth extra, with Six Original Illustrations, 3s. 6d.

Little Bluebird, the Girl Missionary. Square 8vo, cloth, 1s.; cheap edition, 1½d., or 8s. 4d. per 100.

Miss Graham's "Protegs." Square 8vo, cloth, price 1s.

LITTLE BLUEBIRD and MISS GRAHAM'S "PROTEGS." bound together, cloth, 1s. 6d.

Elder Logan's Story about the Kirks. A Book for the Young. Small crown 8vo, cloth extra, Illustrated, 1s. 6d.; paper, 6d.

The "Come" and "Go" Family Text Book. Containing a "COME" and "GO" Text for every day in the year; also spaces for Births, Marriages, and Deaths. Second Thousand. Extra crown 8vo, 5s.; in handsome leather bindings, red and gold rounded corners, 7s. 6d., 8s. 6d., and 10s. 6d.

Bits about America. Paper, 1s.; cloth, 1s. 6d.

EDINBURGH: OLIPHANT, ANDERSON, & FERRI

www.ingramcontent.com/pod-product-compliance
Lightning Source LLC
LaVergne TN
LVHW081346060426
835508LV00017B/1440